THE SERIOUS GARDENER™

RELIABLE
Roses

THE SERIOUS GARDENER™

RELIABLE
Roses

THE NEW YORK BOTANICAL GARDEN

TEXT BY
CHRISTINE UTTERBACK
WITH
MICHAEL RUGGIERO
MASTER GARDENER

FOREWORD BY
GREGORY LONG
SERIES EDITOR:
TOM CHRISTOPHER

CLARKSON POTTER
PUBLISHERS
NEW YORK

PHOTOGRAPH CREDITS

American Rose Society: Page 162L, 172L, 172C. Cathy Wilkinson Barash: 145R. Margery Daughtrey: 148L, 149L. Richard Felber: 9, 12–15, 17–20, 22, 23,181. Pamela Harper: 8, 51L, 52R, 54R, 152. Dency Kane: 2, 28, 38–40, 42, 44–45, 46, 47, 65, 67, 70, 71, 76–83, 87–90, 96, 98, 99, 107, 110–113, 122–124, 131, 154, 155LR, 156, 157R, 158LC, 159LR, 160LR, 161LC, 163C, 164R, 165LR, 166LC, 167LC, 168R, 169LR, 170CR, 171, 172R, 173LC, 174R, 175, 176R, 178R, 179CR, 180R. The New York Botanical Garden Library: 6, 10, 26, 33, 53, 65, 74, 100, 116, 134, 150, 182. Mike Ruggiero: 24, 35, 41, 43, 48, 49, 51R, 52L, 54L, 55, 60, 61, 66, 68, 69, 84, 85, 91, 114, 140, 143, 144, 145L, 146, 147, 148R, 149R, 155C, 157LC, 158R, 159C, 160C, 161R, 162CR, 163LR, 164LC, 165C, 166R, 167R, 168LC, 169C, 170L, 173R, 174LC, 176LC, 177, 178LC, 179L, 180L

Published by Clarkson N. Potter, Inc., 201 East 50th Street, New York, New York 10022. Member of the Crown Publishing Group.

Random House, Inc. New York, Toronto, London, Sydney, Auckland http://www.randomhouse.com/

THE SERIOUS GARDENER, CLARKSON N. POTTER, POTTER, and colophon are trademarks of Clarkson N. Potter, Inc.

Printed in China
Design by Peter Bradford and Danielle Whiteson
Research for the Appendix was conducted by Ken Molinari and Doris Straus.

Library of Congress Cataloging-in-Publication Data

Utterback, Christine.
    Serious gardener series : reliable roses/by The New York Botanical Garden; text by Christine Utterback with Michael Ruggiero, master gardener; foreword by Gregory Long.
    Includes index.
    1. Rose culture. 2. Roses. 3. Roses—Pictorial works.
    I. Ruggiero, Michael. II. New York Botanical Garden.
    III. Title.

SB411.U77   1997
635.9'33372—dc20   96-22102

ISBN 0-609-80086-8
10 9 8 7 6 5 4 3 2 1
First Edition

CONTENTS

FOREWORD

Beatrix Farrand, the now-famous garden designer of the early 1900s, planned the grand rose garden of The New York Botanical Garden in 1916. However, the garden was not built to her specifications until David and Peggy Rockefeller generously funded its construction 71 years later in 1987, and finally senior curator Mike Ruggiero planted it in 1988. From its inception until the present, what is today called the Peggy Rockefeller Rose Garden has represented to many the vision that all four of these "creators" have shared: an insistence that the public deserves the best in garden design and horticulture; a belief that public gardens must be educational experiences; and the happy realization that if gardeners know what they are doing, successful rose-growing is within everyone's reach.

Reliable Roses also shares this combined vision, offering one of the most complete guides to successful rose-growing for the serious home gardener. At The New York Botanical Garden, we have heard over the years that many gardeners have given up on roses. Our students and visitors tell us that their roses aren't as good as they should be, aren't worth the effort, or aren't growing with much success. Mike

Ruggiero, with vast and rich experience in our major rose garden, and with years and years of teaching people to garden (including professionals and students in our School of Professional Horticulture), contributed his authority and knowledge to create a rose handbook useful to gardeners all across the country. Edited by Tom Christopher, himself a distinguished rosarian, *Reliable Roses* includes basic growing information as well as new techniques developed at NYBG, and is born of all of our belief that with the most complete information and knowledge, all gardeners can produce beautiful blooms.

Roses are very ancient plants, both in the New World and in the Old. They have been cultivated for more than 2,000 years, and have been grown on the site of NYBG for nearly 200 years. Today, our Peggy Rockefeller Rose Garden is a virtual encyclopedia of all roses—the varied types and classes, antique and modern, major shrubs and miniatures, tried and untried—all described in detail throughout the book. While it is a beautiful place, inspired by the turn-of-the-century Parisian rose garden Roseraie de l'Hay, it is also a living catalog of what can be grown today at home.

ABOVE: Two centuries have not lessened the appeal of 'Petite de Hollande', a Centifolia rose that originated in the Netherlands circa 1800. A living encyclopedia, the Peggy Rockefeller Rose Garden, OPPOSITE, invites visitors to learn as well as enjoy.

What we have assumed is not that our readers will want to build rose-only gardens, but that they will want to use reliable, hardy, relatively easy roses among the other plants in their gardens, and that they will want to experiment. With the help of these rose authorities, any gardener should be able to have success stories. I hope one day you will be able to visit our gardens and tell us about them yourself.

Gregory Long, President, The New York Botanical Garden

Rose jaune de soufre.   *Rosa sulfurea.*

P. J. Redouté.   Langlois.

INTRODUCTION

In spring and in fall, and through the summer as he can make the time, Michael Ruggiero scrutinizes his roses. They aren't really his roses, of course—Ruggiero himself says that they belong to whoever walks into the garden. At the Peggy Rockefeller Rose Garden of The New York Botanical Garden, that includes a lot of people. Some 15 million people live within an easy drive of these roses, and several million of them are gardeners. Ruggiero's role, as he sees it, is to make their mistakes for them.

There are thousands of roses on the market, and dozens of new cultivars join them each year. All sound appealing in the catalog descriptions, and many really are fine plants. But the rose that looks so attractively compact in the pot at the garden center may explode into a 15-foot shrub that will overrun half your backyard. Or it may attract every passing disease and prove a source of infection to the other roses in your garden. You can't know these things until you have actually tried the plants, and that, according to Mike Ruggiero, is the heart of his job.

That's why he periodically walks through the garden with his checklist, evaluating all the roses. In past years he assessed only the modern roses, but recently he has begun scrutinizing the collection of historical roses in the same way. With the revival of interest in old-fashioned roses, people are buying these antiques again, and they have to know how they too will perform in the garden.

Evaluating for bloom. Ruggiero checks the quality of each rose-bush's bloom: the quantity of flowers, the size of the blossoms, the purity of the colors, and the shape and fragrance of the flowers. He also looks for recurrence of bloom. Because roses bear their flowers in "flushes," or bursts, he wants to know how soon after one flush fades the rosebush will bear another. He cites the example of the pink Hybrid Tea 'Sweet Surrender'—"one of the most fragrant pretty roses you

Created in 1987 from plans dating back to 1918, the Peggy Rockefeller Rose Garden serves as both a graceful and ever-colorful display and an intensive testing ground.

could want. But it takes 8 weeks to come back into flower." There are other roses in the garden that rebloom in as little as $3\frac{1}{2}$ weeks, and that means far more flowers.

Foliage criteria. Foliage quality is important, too. Is the foliage attractive enough that the rosebush is an asset to the garden even when not in bloom? Ruggiero favors roses with red-hued new growth, as the coloring makes a handsome setting for the flowers. Even more important, though, is whether or not the foliage remains clean and healthy; fungal diseases such as powdery mildew, blackspot, and in recent years downy mildew are roses' greatest enemies, and these show themselves first on the foliage. If, despite his program of preventive sprays, a rose proves prone to diseases, Ruggiero records that information, too.

'New Dawn'—the rose sheeting over this gazebo—has proven itself twice as attractive: it is both beautiful and supremely vigorous.

Winter hardiness. Finally, he checks in early spring to see how each rose has weathered the winter. Is that plant hardy? No matter how beautiful a rose may be when in bloom, there's little point in planting it if it will behave like an expensive annual. 'French Lace', for example, the white Floribunda rose introduced onto the market in 1980, bears superb flowers, but in zone 6 it should really be grown only in a greenhouse. Planting 'French Lace' outdoors is one of Mike Ruggiero's mistakes that home gardeners won't have to repeat.

Visitors to the Peggy Rockefeller Rose Garden can pick up a copy of his most recent rose evaluations as they walk through the garden. He tracks each rose, for two full years and keeps the data on a computer, printing out a new summary annually as part of his efforts to make this garden (as he puts it) "user-friendly." That's also why he has, for the most part, avoided rarities in the planting of this collection.

Ruggiero enjoys visiting what he calls "connoisseur gardens," rose gardens whose owners pride themselves on having roses no one else grows. But he believes that such a collection is frustrating to average gardeners—it inspires in them a desire for plants they probably cannot obtain. The Peggy Rockefeller Rose Garden's primary role is to exhibit the best of the roses that home gardeners will find in mail-order catalogs and at garden centers.

ABOVE: Modern landscape rose 'Carefree Wonder' blooms the same year after year, with only occasional spring pruning and no winter protection. OPPOSITE: Hybrid Musk roses embracing a bench offer subtler pleasures in the garden.

Scented rose varietals. He also strives to demonstrate the range of roses that can be had within any one class. In the last few years, for instance, he has been planting a bed of fragrant Floribunda roses. Many rosarians complain that modern roses have lost their scent, but Ruggiero has collected 16 highly perfumed Floribunda cultivars—all modern roses— and plans to add 3 more. His goal is not only to prove a point but also to suggest what is possible. For by planting these 19 very diverse shrubs together, he hopes to show visitors the range of flower colors and shapes they can have while still enjoying a heady perfume.

A HERITAGE OF ROSES

Through his research, Mike Ruggiero is passing along to visitors the knowledge he has gained through 32 years of rose growing. He began as a high school student, when he first hired on at The New York Botanical Garden for a summer job. He was casual labor then, and the gardeners didn't trust him to do more than weed or deadhead (which

means to clip off the faded blossoms.) But he returned summer after summer, eventually coming to work at the botanical garden full-time after finishing school. Through the years he has worked in every one of the garden's plant collections. Roses, though, have been an ongoing interest, and a major responsibility since 1980, when he was given supervision of the rose garden. Today, as senior curator, he oversees every aspect of the care of 2,700 plants of some 255 rose species and cultivars.

In the hands of Mike Ruggiero and the other NYBG gardeners, this garden has become a marvelous combination of laboratory and teaching tool. But the shape of the garden, its character and the quality of its bloom, owes much to past gardeners, too. The New York Botanical Garden has been growing roses longer than almost any other public garden in America. Indeed, there was a rose garden on this site well before there was a New York Botanical Garden.

Beginnings of the NYBG rose garden. Although it isn't clear exactly when roses were first planted in this area just to the east of the Bronx River, by the 1840s the "acre of roses" here was already locally renowned. The land belonged to tobacco merchant Pierre Lorillard. Lorillard had built a mansion and outbuildings on the property, but his main interest was in its commercial potential: here the Bronx River runs through a gorge, creating an ideal site for a water-powered mill. This mill (which still stands) ground tobacco into snuff, at that time a fashionable product. The roses Lorillard planted in extensive beds right by the mill were an essential part of the manufacturing process, harvested to be mixed with snuff to make it more appealing to the nose.

It is not known what kinds of roses grew in that first planting, but they must have been highly perfumed, hardy shrubs, almost certainly specimens of the primitive classes known as Damask and Gallica roses. Like most of the old-fashioned roses, these bloom heavily just once a season, bearing large crops of flowers in late spring or early summer. Despite their failure to rebloom, they still deserve the place they have in NYBG's present rose garden, because they are sturdy, long-lived bushes, many of which also bear handsome and disease-resistant foliage. And they are valuable for their historical importance as ancestors of our modern roses.

NYBG's founding director, Nathaniel Lord Britton, must have had little predilection for such an uneducational garden. Though roses were, along with a "Fruticetum" for fruiting plants, a "Vinetum" for vines, and a "Pinetum" for conifers, part of his plans for the institution he helped found in 1896, Britton's vision of a rose garden called for a living textbook, a carefully designed display of the different sorts and classes available to gardeners in the Northeast.

This new garden opened in April 1913, and while it was better ordered than its predecessor, it was also a more modest affair: instead of an acre of roses, Britton contented himself with a single 250-foot-long, 8-foot-wide bed. Still, it included some 140 kinds of roses, with representatives of what were then the half dozen most popular classes.

The spot under the sassafras tree on an adjacent hill is the best vantage point to study the system of beds that landscape designer Beatrix Farrand created as NYBG's living textbook of roses.

As well as the Hybrid Tea roses familiar to modern gardeners, there were also Hybrid Perpetuals and Tea roses (parents of the Hybrid Teas), Polyantha roses, Moss roses, and Bourbon roses. Notably lacking were the modest but highly scented flowers that had been the mainstay of the Lorillard garden. By 1913 those old-fashioned shrubs were no longer to be found in nursery catalogs.

Historical roses. Until just a few years ago, classic roses, the exquisite old cultivars that had built the popularity of this flower, were virtually unobtainable in the United States. Fashions change in roses as regularly as they do in cars or clothes, and as older rose cultivars dropped out of favor, the nurserymen likewise dropped them from the catalogs. Few gardeners even realized that something was being lost, since public gardens seldom displayed the older "unimproved" roses. When The New York Botanical Garden installed a large and comprehensive exhibit of historical roses in 1969, it helped to reawaken the public interest in rose antiques and spur a revival in their popularity. Today, of course, there are dozens of nurseries that specialize in the production and sale of the so-called old-fashioned roses, and many of the finer types are available even at the better garden centers.

ABOVE: The NYBG was a pioneer in reintroducing Old Garden roses to the public. OPPOSITE: Chains hung between posts serve as display cases for climbers such as the light pink 'Clair Matin' and the darker 'Malaga'. FOLLOWING PAGE: As in the Peggy Rockefeller Rose Garden, clusters of the Modern Shrub rose 'Bonica' comprise a colorful, informal hedge.

Serving as the eyes and ears of the nursery industry in this way is, according to Mike Ruggiero, another part of the Peggy Rockefeller Rose Garden's mission. Every year he plants in the garden the All-America Rose Selection committee's choices from the rose cultivars

newly introduced onto the market—these AARS winners are the roses that the nursery industry thinks will be most popular. But Ruggiero and the other NYBG gardeners are always talking to visitors, too, finding out from them which roses they truly like. And this information he passes back to the nurserymen with whom he deals and whom he meets at shows and conferences. That helps to keep the rose hybridizers and the nurserymen in touch with what the home gardener wants, enabling the professionals to better target their production.

"Don't try to impose your taste," Ruggiero maintains. "Show people what they can grow, what will do well for them, and let them make a choice." The Peggy Rockefeller Rose Garden's role is to help make sure the choice is an informed one.

THE GARDEN TODAY

In its present form the NYBG's rose garden is very much a new one—and yet it is also more than three generations old. The design of the garden is a classic. It was drafted in 1918 by Beatrix Farrand, one of the 20th-century's greatest landscape architects, and the only woman among the founding members of the American Society of Landscape Architects. Farrand's plans for the NYBG rose garden were considered too expensive when originally presented to the botanical garden's board—they would have cost $10,000 to realize. By 1987 the cost had risen to $1 million, but NYBG had found a most generous donor, David Rockefeller, who supplied the necessary funds to create Farrand's garden as a tribute to his wife, Peggy.

The Peggy Rockefeller Rose Garden today. The latest incarnation of the rose garden, the Peggy Rockefeller Rose Garden, is not only a laboratory where roses are tested but also (in the Britton tradition) a living textbook. There are roses of 23 different classes, old and new, with each class displayed in its own area. Different ways to grow roses are also displayed: roses climb pergolas and fences, spread out in formal beds, and rise up on straight, single trunks to make treelike "standards." There are huge, expansive shrubs that grow more than head high—shrubs that would suit only the largest home gardens. There are

Miniature roses, too, bushes that reach a height of only 18 inches or less and bear perfect blossoms often no bigger than a quarter. There is, as the garden's creators intended, a good selection from which visitors can pick the rose that pleases them, and there is a rose here to please almost anyone.

Certainly roses should be a pleasure to grow. This flower has reigned over the American garden since its beginnings, even long before Pierre Lorillard planted his acre of roses. The rose is a floral symbol of the United States and remains far and away our most popular flower—we harvest more than a billion buds (exactly 1,205,832,000, according to the most recent figures) annually just to fill vases and to fashion into boutonnieres.

Reliable roses. Yet in recent years gardeners have been turning away from roses, complaining that they are too difficult to grow, too unreliable, and naturally unhealthy. Who wants a plant that must be dosed constantly with toxic chemicals? Anyway, all roses look alike, don't they? And the tall, twiggy, disease-prone plants at the garden center don't seem to blend well with other plants—who wants a bush that must be segregated off in its own private bed?

These are questions that Mike Ruggiero hears often, and his answer is to point to the Peggy Rockefeller Rose Garden. Roses can be healthy, reliable shrubs, and they offer tremendous diversity of flower, size, and foliage. Roses don't have to keep to themselves, either; with all the forms these shrubs can take, there are any number of roles they can play in the home landscape—especially in the hands of a knowledgeable gardener.

A border of blue-blossomed, silver-leaved catmint visually unites the diverse flowers in the Old Garden rose section.

HOW THIS BOOK IS ORGANIZED

Mike Ruggiero is not only a master gardener, he's also an experienced and enthusiastic teacher who shares his knowledge of gardening in the classroom as well as in the field. This book is, essentially, his master class in rose gardening.

From his years of testing, Ruggiero knows that roses can be reliable and self-sufficient shrubs—if the gardener knows how to find the roses suited to his or her situation. Even experienced rose growers need to take a second look at the new types coming onto the market and the renewed availability of classic roses.

A basic knowledge of gardening is assumed throughout this book, but in many cases fundamental information about planting and pruning has been included because rose-growing techniques differ somewhat from those that apply to other types of shrubs. Even experienced gardeners need to review the basics when taking up roses for the first time. Every master gardener, like every master chef, has his or her own tricks of the trade, and they often make the difference between good and excellent results.

In the space of a short walk, one can experience roses of 23 different classes, such as climbing roses 'Red Fountain', swarming up a pillar, and beyond those, a bed of miniature roses.

Chapter 1 presents a review of rose ancestors of the many classes of cultivated roses and explores the reasons why these less common plants often outperform the ubiquitous Hybrid Teas.

Chapter 2 helps readers choose roses that are best suited to their own particular gardens, by describing the needs and strengths of different rose classes, as well as the process of analyzing soil type, exposure, and the other aspects of the landscape and climate that determine what roses will flourish on a site.

Chapter 3 offers insights into designing a rose garden and on integrating roses into other types of garden plantings, from the formal to informal, as hedges or container plantings, and as companions for herbs and perennials, noting the beauties of the rose's foliage and fruits, and even its thorns.

The source of a rosebush determines its type and condition, and in turn how it must be planted. Chapter 4 advises gardeners how to enter the specialized world of rose nurseries as knowledgeable shoppers, equipped to select not only roses of the type best suited to their needs but also the healthiest specimens. Mike Ruggiero also shares the procedures he has developed for getting different kinds of rosebushes—bare-rooted, potted, and boxed—off to a good start.

Rosarians have tended to treat rose pruning like a ritual, offering the uninitiated detailed prescriptions that often seem mutually contradictory. Chapter 5 describes a simple system based on the growth habits of the different rose classes, and discusses overwatering practices.

Chapter 6 deals with the issue that more than any other has driven

On a sunny day in June, visitors flock to the Peggy Rockefeller Rose Garden—to study, compare, and above all enjoy curator Mike Ruggiero's reliable roses.

modern gardeners away from roses: pest and disease control. Fewer and fewer gardeners are willing to make constant applications of toxic chemicals. Acceptance may be the appropriate response to some levels of insect infestation; consistency and an insider's knowledge should govern the response to diseases.

In **Chapter 7** readers will find photographs and descriptions of 80 roses that have proven especially reliable and rewarding in the Peggy Rockefeller Rose Garden at the NYBG. Besides serving as a directory of beautiful and hardy cultivars, this list also provides clues that will assist gardeners on further searches, for in the descriptions of the 80 extra-reliable roses are the names of the hybridizers and nurseries who bred them. By searching for other creations from the same sources, readers may get a head start on expanding their personal rose list.

Appendix: The Best and the Worst. Those who garden in regions distant from The New York Botanical Garden will find in the appendix clues to the best roses for their area, as well as the most serious problems they will encounter. "The Best and the Worst" section is a survey that features information about the 10 best-performing roses and the worst cultural problems encountered at 27 public rose gardens across the United States.

Throughout these chapters, the emphasis is on personal experience, for the craft embodied in that is the greatest gift one gardener can give to another. Mike Ruggiero has grown hundreds of rose species and cultivars, yet his perspective is not that of the connoisseur who disdains the amateur's efforts. "I long ago realized this isn't my garden," he says. "My garden at home has what I like, but the Peggy Rockefeller Rose Garden is for everybody. The more people we can reach, the more we ask what they want and then give it to them, the more people will come here, and the more people will learn, and the more people will be happy. What else do you need?"

With this book, The New York Botanical Garden introduces the best tips from one of its most respected master gardeners, in the hope that every gardener can become a bit of a master in the field Mike Ruggiero best loves.

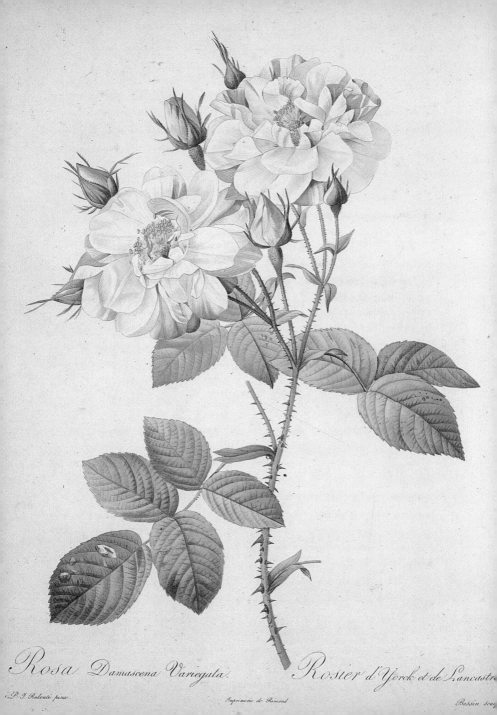

Rosa Damascena Variegata.   *Rosier d'Yorck et de Lancastre.*

P. J. Redouté pinx.   Imprimerie de Rémond.   Bessin sculp.

1
BLOODLINES AND BIRTHRIGHTS

"This weed . . . is found in pastures, fence rows, and clearings and along the borders of woods and roadsides. . . . May be destroyed by persistent mechanical cutting and physically removing the roots from the soil with an ax and shovel, or by applying a foliar spray of glyphosate or picloram or a mixture of 2,4–D and dicamba repeated as necessary. In West Virginia 36,500 ha [90,200 acres] are infested, with more than 9,000 ha [22,000 acres] heavily infested . . . control [is] expected to cost $40 million over a 10-year period." (From Weeds of the United States and Their Control *by Harri J. Lorenzi and Larry S. Jeffery, 1987, p. 167.)*

hat weed is this? Is it kudzu or poison ivy? In fact, the tenacious plant featured in this passage from a standard guide to weeds is a rose, a member of the genus *Rosa*. It is the wild rose, *R. multiflora,* a Chinese species that was introduced into this country for use as a hedge plant. Forty years ago this rose was distributed to farmers as a "living fence" by the Department of Agriculture. Clearly over the intervening decades, it has gotten out of hand.

The point is that roses can be healthy, tough, and reliable plants. As garden plants, they have developed a reputation for being finicky and delicate, and many modern cultivars (types of roses developed in cultivation) do fit that profile. But others don't. Many of the wild roses—what rosarians such as The New York Botanical Garden's Mike Ruggiero call "species roses"—are among the toughest, most adaptable shrubs there are. Many are handsome, desirable plants as well.

Rosa rugosa. In the most exposed, rocky areas on the islands off the coast of Maine, outcrops that are underwater when spring tides flood, you will find flourishing specimens of *R. rugosa,* another import from Asia that has gone wild throughout northeastern North America. From early summer into fall, these bushes bear pink to purplish flowers 3 inches across, and after these fade, each blossom is replaced by a fat red fruit, a "hip" as big as a crab apple. The dark green, crinkled

Few garden shrubs flourish in the tough conditions of the seaside, yet the hardy Rosa rugosa's *excellent growth proves that luxury can be found in unusual places.*

foliage is virtually disease-proof, and in autumn the leaves turn an attractive yellow before dropping. Winter temperatures as low as −40°F won't damage a healthy specimen of *R. rugosa.*

R. rugosa is sold by many mail-order nurseries and is sometimes found in the better local garden centers, too. At the NYBG it grows on the hill overlooking the Peggy Rockefeller Rose Garden, and it is one of the few roses in the garden that never need spraying for diseases or pests. And *R. rugosa* is not the only reliable rose that is also beautiful.

But if the wild roses are such hardy plants, why are modern garden roses so often anything but? To understand that we need to follow the rose's history from its free and easy beginnings to its position as the plant kingdom's version of the modern pedigreed dog, fraught with flaws from breeding that however well meaning has defeated nature's law of survival of the fittest.

IN FROM THE WILD

Of course, roses long predate their first use as garden plants: fossils excavated from rock deposits in Oregon, Colorado, Alaska, and Japan show with some accuracy that roses have been blooming in those places for some 35 million years. Long before the appearance of the first human being, roses were flourishing throughout the Northern Hemisphere, with major concentrations of species in Europe, Asia, the Middle East, and America. Curiously, no evidence exists that roses grew anywhere south of the equator until humans brought them there. But roses grew nearly everywhere in the northern half of the globe in an impressive diversity. Botanists have identified some 250 distinct species, and these range from brawny monsters like the subtropical *R. gigantea* of southern China and Burma, which bears 5½-inch-wide blossoms of creamy white on canes that may climb to 30 feet; to *R. acicularis,* the arctic rose, a species of the far north that makes a shrub 3 feet tall, with bristly stems, 2-inch-wide bright pink blossoms, and orange, pear-shaped hips.

In general, these wild roses share a number of characteristics. They tend to be thorny, and all are shrubs—even the so-called climbing roses are actually shrubs with long, flexible shoots rather than true climbers or vines. The leaves are pinnately compound, with each leaf divided into three or more leaflets arranged in featherlike fashion around a central stem. The flowers may be big or small, but they commonly have five petals, and they tend to be fragrant. The flowers are followed by fleshy red or orange fruits—hips—that, though smaller, clearly reveal the rose's close relationship to the apple.

Antecedents of modern roses. Though the rose was first domesticated in Europe and Asia, most of our modern garden roses descend from Old World species. North America is, actually, unusually rich in roses. As many as 170 species of roses have been identified as native to this continent. None of these species has played a prominent role in the breeding programs of rose hybridizers. But many are fine plants in their own right and are well worth growing.

When gardeners began cultivating roses is, of course, unknown, although archaeologists have found proof that the rose was a favorite flower as long ago as 3000 B.C. A highly detailed piece of golden jewelry from that period that was recovered from a Sumerian ruin in the Middle East depicts a ram caught in a thornbush that is sprouting a flower clearly intended to represent a rose. To the west, on the island of Crete, archaeologists have found a palace mural dating from about 1700 B.C. in which five-petaled pink roses figure. The models for both these artworks were wild roses—or at least they were indistinguishable from wild roses. But then, the first garden roses must surely have been bushes dug out of a wild thicket.

The first written description of rose gardening dates to the 4th century A.D., and it is interesting because it emphasizes how tough and self-reliant the garden roses of that era were. The description is found in the very first botanical handbook, *Inquiry into Plants* by the Greek scientist Theophrastus. Though Theophrastus demonstrates a knowledge of starting roses from seed, he recommends starting new bushes from cuttings, as that method of propagation is much faster. As to caring for rosebushes, his recommendation is brutal but effective: "A rosebush lives five years, after which its prime is past, unless pruned by burning. With this plant also the flower becomes inferior with age."

Burning the whole bush to the ground would force out a flush of new growth and also fertilize the surrounding soil with ashes. It would, in addition, cleanse the bush of insect pests and any fungal diseases that had attacked the foliage. But only the hardiest of plants could survive this treatment.

As gardeners' horticultural skills increased, less drastic methods of rose maintenance were developed—the ancient Romans perfected the art of rose grafting and even devised ways to force roses into flower out of season, pouring hot water around their roots to keep them growing through the Italian winter. Yet garden roses remained vigorous plants, outstanding performers that could, for the most part, take care of themselves. Ancient writings on roses never

Theophrastus's recommendation is brutal: "A rosebush lives five years, after which its prime is past, unless pruned by burning."

mention whether or not a particular bush was healthy and hardy; it was assumed that rosebushes would be. This, no doubt, was because the plants continued to be essentially specimens of the hardy, wild species that gardeners found growing locally.

Early rose selection. Often the garden roses were unusually fine examples of the wild roses. Even in ancient times, gardeners watched for flowers that were exceptionally large, or double (bearing twice or many times the normal complement of five petals). They treasured flowers of uncommon hue. Western gardeners were particularly covetous of this color variety, since the rose species native to Europe naturally bore flowers only in shades of red, pink, or white; yellow was a color long sought but mostly absent from Western roses until modern times. Western gardeners also watched for roses that bloomed more than once in a year, as most of their native species produced just one flush of flowers in late spring or early summer. Any rose that would rebloom (now called a "remontant" rose) was prized. Ancient Roman gardeners in the vicinity of the Italian town of Paestum succeeded in collecting such a plant, a rose that produced a second flush of flowers in the fall, and it was famous throughout the ancient world. Indeed, growing roses for the floral trade became the main industry of the region surrounding Paestum, so that roses gradually forced every other crop out of the local farmers' fields.

In short, ancient gardeners valued most of the same things in roses that modern gardeners do: size, quality, and color of bloom; fragrance; and the freedom with which a plant flowered. But because they did not understand the mechanics by which plants produce seeds, they never mastered the art of hybridization. Modern horticulturists force change onto the plants through calculated crosses of one plant with another. Ancient gardeners could only wait and watch.

When a particularly fine plant appeared in the garden, perhaps as the result of a spontaneous mutation or perhaps as the result of a spontaneous cross between roses of two species that happened to be planted next to each other, the ancient gardeners seized on the superior offspring. They understood vegetative propagation: that by taking a piece of a superior bush and either rooting it as a cutting or grafting it onto the roots of some other rose, they could create new bushes identical to the parent. In this way, the ancients gradually amassed a small collection of distinguished rose cultivars: one ancient Roman book, *Natural History* by Pliny the Elder, lists 13 named varieties.

Growing ancient roses today. Incidentally, at least one of the ancient Roman roses is probably still grown in modern gardens. The twice-blooming rose of Paestum (formerly classified as *R. × damascena* 'Bifera') has been identified as one of the roses classed today 'Autumn Damask'. Specimens of these are perfectly winter-hardy in zone 6 and flourish in the Peggy Rockefeller Rose Garden.

'Autumn Damask' may be the only authentically Roman rose at the NYBG, but there are plenty of other roses of ancient types. Among the old garden roses grown in the Peggy Rockefeller Rose Garden are other Damask roses; Gallica roses, which descend from the native European species *R. gallica*, Alba roses, descended from the native European rose *R. × alba*; and Centifolia roses (often called "cabbage roses" because of the size of their blossoms and the number of petals) which trace their ancestry to a very old European rose, *R. × centifolia*, which may be a true species or may have originated in crosses of two or more wild roses of different species.

Botanical diversity. The diversity of these old garden roses' parentage was another secret of why roses continued to perform so reliably for many centuries after they were transplanted. Each species brought with it into the garden an adaptation to different soils and climates, and their immediate offspring typically continued to show these strengths. Because the ancient roses included mixtures of all sorts of different species, gardeners could almost always find among them a rose that was suited to their garden's conditions. And a rosebush that finds itself in conditions it likes is naturally more vigorous and less likely to fall prey to insects or diseases or to need special coddling in the form of winter protection. In short, a well-adapted rose is a healthy, carefree rose.

French painter Pierre-Joseph Redouté captures in his 19th-century portrait the classic beauty of the 'Autumn Damask', a plant that still delights visitors to the NYBG rose garden.

This art of matching rose type to garden is lost to most modern gardeners. Today we tend to select from just one or two classes of roses: Hybrid Tea and Floribunda roses currently account for the overwhelming majority of sales. These two classes of roses include many fine cultivars, but they cannot succeed everywhere. It is only in the last decade or so that American gardeners have learned again to look farther afield, to roses of other, often ancient classes. If your roses fail to flourish, it may be that you are not giving them adequate care, but it may also be that the roses are just poorly adapted to your conditions.

Why did gardeners lose sight of diversity's importance? Why did they stop breeding for reliable roses?

Arrival of Asian roses in Europe. Two discoveries redirected the course of rose history, almost simultaneously. In the late 18th century, gardeners in Europe discovered the basic techniques of hybridization. Flower growers in the Netherlands were apparently the first to find ways to promote the crossing of related species and cultivars and so produce offspring with characteristics of both parents on demand. At the same time, the China trade introduced new species of roses from Asia, primarily from China, to Europeans, who found one feature in particular of the new roses very exciting. The Asian roses tended to be far less winter-hardy than the native European species (most will not thrive in North America north of zone 8), but whereas the European roses for the most part produced only one flush of flowers each year, the Chinese roses rebloomed repeatedly, producing new flowers as long as the weather remained warm.

These exotic flowers, the first truly "everblooming" roses, would not overwinter in northern Europe outside of greenhouses and so were of limited use to gardeners. But rose nurserymen realized that by hybridizing, by crossing the Chinese roses with their cold-hardy European relatives, they could produce new classes of garden roses that would flower in an English, French, or German garden from late spring until late fall. Almost immediately, a host of new rose classes appeared: China roses, Tea roses (so called because of a fancied resemblance of the flowers' perfume to the aroma of tea leaves), Noisette roses, Portland roses, Bourbon roses, Hybrid Perpetual roses, and eventually (in the late 19th century) the first Hybrid Tea roses.

Creating the first hybrids. The creation of truly everblooming winter-hardy roses was a slow process. Each new class tended to bloom more freely and over a longer period than those that came before, but only with the Hybrid Teas, after almost a century of crosses, did rose hybridizers achieve what they had set out to do. In the Hybrid Tea, the hybridizers had produced bushes that bore flowers of spectacular size and bushes that rebloomed as freely as any of the Asian ancestors. The problem was that the hybridizers reached this goal by repeatedly crossing the most everblooming of garden cultivars. Gradually they bred the diversity out of roses. As the hybridizers moved further and further away from the wild ancestors, the roses slowly lost much of the wild roses' toughness and vigor.

New rose colors. The last big step in the evolution of the modern garden rose was to broaden the palette of colors. In 1900 a French nursery introduced onto the market a rose called 'Soleil d'Or', a bush with rich orange-yellow blossoms, a color previously unknown in winter-hardy roses. The breeder had produced this by crossing a European

Despite its demure appearance, 'La France', generally accepted as the first Hybrid Tea rose, sparked a revolution when it appeared in 1867.

garden rose of the Hybrid Perpetual class with a Middle Eastern rose: *R. foetida* 'Persiana', the Persian Yellow rose. The was Persian Yellow contributed the genes for yellow flowers, but unfortunately this rose also passed along a severe susceptibility to the fungal disease blackspot. Other nurserymen began using 'Soleil d'Or' as a parent in their breeding programs and with it managed to create the luminous flower colors that delight modern rose growers. At the same time, though, they spread susceptibility to disease throughout the Hybrid Tea roses and the classes that descend from them: the Floribunda and Grandiflora roses.

Problems with modern roses. It is important to emphasize that many Hybrid Tea, Floribunda, and Grandiflora roses are healthy plants. But as a group they are considerably less hardy and healthy than the roses of long ago. Contributing to this trend has been the increasing sophistication in rose maintenance: as chemical pesticides and fungicides became available, gardeners could successfully cultivate plants that would not survive unprotected. The cost of these chemical cures has been that today's gardeners concerned with environmental hazards have shunned roses altogether. Mike Ruggiero understands this: "In the overall scheme of things, how do you justify poisoning a whole environment in order to create one plant of beauty? You have to strike a balance there." But besides its harmful impact on the environment, the increasing need for sprays over the last century has made roses more and more work and less fun to grow.

> *The point is, roses can be healthy, tough, and reliable plants. Many of the wild roses, or "species roses," are among the toughest shrubs.*

Fortunately, this is changing. Ruggiero says that the appearance of an increasing number of what are commonly billed as "landscape roses" is proof that hybridizers have gotten the message. These landscape roses such as 'Bonica' and 'Carefree Wonder' (described on page 163) are Modern Shrub roses that are advertised as nearly disease- and pest-proof, and in fact he has found that to be true in many cases. He is also intrigued with the compact Rugosa hybrids, the "Pavement" roses that rose breeders in Germany have been introducing onto the market. From 2½ to 3 feet tall, these mounded shrubs have preserved the wild Rugosa's hardiness, but they offer double flowers in shades ranging from pure white to red and purple.

Disease resistance and hardiness among the Hybrid Teas, Floribundas, and Grandifloras remain erratic. Ruggiero finds that these properties continue to vary widely in his new acquisitions. But from his records emerge several cultivars that are eminently healthy, practical bushes (descriptions of these will be found in the guide to his favorite roses in chapter 7).

Meanwhile, as Ruggiero points out, more and more gardeners are rediscovering the diversity and toughness of the old-fashioned classes of roses, and as a result nurserymen are making them available to the public again. Whereas 25 years ago The New York Botanical Garden maintained one of only a very few collections of old-fashioned roses in the New York City area, now shrubs of this type are to be seen in many public and private gardens.

Old or new, healthy roses are finding their way back into our gardens. As they do, this garden standby will recapture its old popularity. But there will be a difference: the healthy roses will not only be returning to the rose garden but will also be moving out into the landscape to serve in ways roses haven't in the past.

MODERN ROSES

The modern age in rose growing began with the appearance of the first Hybrid Tea rose ('La France') in 1867; that class and the Floribunda and Grandiflora roses that sprang from it swept virtually every other kind of rose from the garden within a couple of generations. Modern roses are typified by an everblooming habit and by a broad range of flower colors, which includes practically every hue except a true blue.

Hybrid Tea roses. This class of roses originated from a series of crosses of Tea roses (a class descended from everblooming Asian species and so not hardy in the North) with the hardier Hybrid Perpetuals. The result was a class of moderately hardy, vigorous shrubs that inherited Tea roses' everblooming habit.

Inbreeding has endowed Hybrid Tea roses like 'Paradise' with perfect forms and glorious, various colors. But the process often robs these roses of their natural vigor.

Hybrid Teas typically bear long, pointed buds on long stems that are ideal for cutting. Inbreeding has given their flowers a remarkable perfection of form and spectacular colors, but it has also robbed many Hybrid Teas of disease resistance and winter hardiness. Owing to their long popularity, more than 6,000 Hybrid Tea roses have been named and registered with the American Rose Society. By choosing wisely from this mass, it is possible to have Hybrid Teas of outstanding vigor and reliability.

Because Hybrid Tea roses respond well to severe pruning (indeed, this treatment improves the size and quality of the flowers, though it reduces their number), these shrubs are excellent for plant-

'Escapade' exhibits all the virtues of the Floribunda rose: superior winter hardiness and resistance to disease coupled with a most generous profusion of blooms.

ing in numbers together in a formal bedding scheme. Hybrid Tea blossoms are the cut flower par excellence. ['Chrysler Imperial'; 'Jardins de Bagatelle'; 'Touch of Class']

Floribunda roses. Floribundas are a relatively new group of roses. Introduced in 1930, the original Floribundas were the result of crosses of Hybrid Tea roses with an old-fashioned class of dwarf roses known as Polyanthas. The result has been a race of relatively compact bushes with superior hardiness and disease resistance that produce large clusters of somewhat smaller blossoms. The Floribunda roses are everblooming and have the classic flower form and wide range of flower colors typical of the Hybrid Teas. Floribunda roses are excellent for bedding displays and will blend well into a mixed border of flowers and shrubs. They are especially valuable for their ability to adapt to a wide range of temperature and soil conditions. ['Sunprite']

'Europeana', a Floribunda rose, is recommended for bedding displays yet looks equally good when interplanted individually as shrubs among perennial flowers.

Hybrid Rugosa roses. This is actually a class of 19th-century origin, but the potential of *R. rugosa* as a parent for a class of hardy, everblooming shrub roses was recognized only a few decades ago.

Since then a number of breeding programs have begun producing cold- and drought-resistant shrub roses that combine the disease-proof, handsomely wrinkled foliage of the Rugosa with a wider variety of flower form and color. Two outstanding strains are the Canadian Explorer Series and the "Pavement" roses from Germany; these last are notably compact (to 2½ or 3 feet tall) and bear double flowers of white, pink, red, or purple. ['Blanc Double de Coubert'; 'Frau Dagmar Hartopp']

Grandiflora roses. This class's name was a term coined in 1954 in the United States as a way to describe a new variety of roses developed by crossing Hybrid Tea and Floribunda roses. Grandifloras owe their flower form and straight, long stems to the Hybrid Tea rose, and their increased hardiness and abundance of continuously blooming flowers to the Floribunda parent. Grandiflora blooms are usually double but lack a striking fragrance. 'Queen Elizabeth' was the first rose to be called Grandiflora and continues to be a good performer in the Peggy Rockefeller Rose Garden.

Miniature roses. A variety of dwarf roses have been cultivated over the years and seem to have been a favorite of imperial Chinese gardeners. The modern Miniature roses, however, are a product of 20th-

ABOVE: 'Frau Dagmar Hartopp' rises up from behind an edging of nepeta at The New York Botanical Garden. OPPOSITE: Hybrid Rugosa roses keep the strength of their wild ancestors while producing a more refined style of blossom.

century European and American breeding programs and date mostly from after World War II.

Miniature rosebushes range in height from 3 to 18 inches, and though their flowers are perfectly formed, they may be no larger than a quarter. The foliage is similarly delicate, in scale with the size of the bushes.

The best of the Miniatures are hardy, free-flowering, and reliable rebloomers. They offer all the flower colors of other modern rose classes and are ideal for use as container plantings; they also integrate easily into rock gardens and make good edgings for beds of larger plants, especially when planted as miniature hedges. There are also a number of climbing Miniatures. ['Candy Sunblaze'; 'Debut'; 'Magic Carrousel']

Modern Shrub roses. This class—which includes most of the so-called landscape roses—is a somewhat miscellaneous one, but it comprises a number of roses that are remarkable for the well-rounded form of the shrubs, for their hardiness, and for the healthiness of their foliage; the majority are very free bloomers as well, producing a good supply of flowers throughout the growing season.

These are shrubs that were bred for planting outside the rose garden in the landscape at large; depending on their size, the Modern Shrub roses may blend well into a mixed border of flowers and shrubs, and they are outstanding material for an informal flowering hedge. ['Bonica';

ABOVE: One of the most popular of the Modern Shrub roses, 'Bonica' possesses disease-resistance and a free-blooming habit on a nicely formed shrub. OPPOSITE: The Miniature rose 'Lady Sunblaze'.

'Cardinal Hume'; 'Carefree Beauty'; 'Carefree Wonder'; 'Fritz Nobis'; 'Nymphenburg'; 'Pink Meidiland'; 'Robusta'; 'Sparrieshoop']

David Austin English roses. While not officially recognized as a class as yet, this remarkable group of roses has won tremendous popularity in the gardening world over the last few years by combining old-fashioned fragrance and charm with a modern reblooming habit. Those grown in the Peggy Rockefeller Rose Garden demonstrate the variety of flower forms—from cupped- to saucer-shaped or almost globular—and the wide range of flower colors to be found among the English roses. ['Abraham Darby'; 'Evelyn'; 'Gertrude Jekyll'; 'Graham Thomas']

ABOVE: Mating old and new characteristics, the English rose 'Graham Thomas' bears blossoms with a rich antique rose perfume, and a luminous hue unknown among the hardy roses of yesteryear. OPPOSITE: 'Abraham Darby', another David Austin English rose.

The same roses found by the first gardeners thousands of years ago growing in a meadow or along a riverbank can still be grown today. "Species roses," as modern gardeners call them, are commonly nothing more than wild bushes transplanted into the garden, although most gardeners purchase them from nurseries rather than venturing out into the wild to collect their own stock. In addition, rosarians often include among the species roses a few types that first appeared in cultivated settings but that are similar to their wild ancestors in most respects and which are believed to be genetically close to the wild types.

As a rule, species roses bear "single" flowers—that is, simple rounds of five petals—and they bloom only for a period of a few weeks, generally during the summer. Of course, wild roses, subject to natural mutations, offer a number of exceptions to these rules. For example, *R. sericea pteracantha* and its close relative, *R. sericea omeiensis*, bear flowers of four petals. And several types of species roses bear the typical flush of flowers in spring or early summer and then again, albeit sporadically, throughout the growing season.

For the most part, species roses tend to be prickly, fragrant, and healthy without any coddling on the

A sport of a wild Middle Eastern species, the Austrian copper rose (Rosa foetida bicolor) *inherited natural charm—and an unpleasant odor—from its parent.*

gardener's part. "Nature's unspoiled children . . . accustomed to neglect" is the description given by one famous rosarian. These unspoiled children are remarkable for their resistance to pests and diseases and for the handsome effects their fruit and foliage lend to the landscape. Species roses are also undemanding plants in that they rarely require pruning except for the occasional removal of a dead cane; an old and overgrown specimen may sometimes benefit from a hard cutting back that encourages the production of fresh and more compact growth.

Although the species types bear less spectacular blossoms than their domesticated relatives, the wild roses have always had their fanciers, mainly because they are such tough, resilient beauties. Bobbink & Atkins, a famous New Jersey nursery that was a strong supporter of the NYBG rose garden, donating thousands of bushes in the early decades of the 20th century, listed 85 species of wild roses in its 1938 catalog. No single nursery today offers such a considerable collection of species roses, but they are beginning to reappear in catalogs.

A number of species roses flourish in the Peggy Rockefeller Rose Garden, though a lack of space and the emphasis on cultivated roses have limited the size of the garden's collection. As Mike Ruggiero puts it, "Although we don't grow many true species roses, we do grow some. Carolina [*R. carolina*] we grow, because it's a native rose, and it actually takes a bit more abuse." This

From the mountains of Persia, Rosa moschata *'Nastarana' survives fierce winter weather, usually returning to bloom even when killed to the ground.*

is a good landscape shrub that he recommends to home gardeners.

"Also we grow eglanteria [*R. eglanteria*], the apothecary rose [*R. gallica officinalis*], *R. hugonis,* and *R. moyesii.* Primula [*R. primula*] we have in a pot, and we have *R. roxburghii* [the chestnut rose], *R. rubrifolia* (*glauca* is its new name), and *R. rugosa.* We also grow some of the hybrid spinosissimas [*R. spinosissima*]. Wichuraiana [*R. wichuraiana*] we have all over the hillside.

Exhibiting a big collection of species roses is just not as important for my public. I like *R. hugonis.* It even turns a good yellow fall color. A monster shrub at 12 feet across it's big for a border, but it has small flowers. NYBG's *R. hugonis* has delicate, almost ferny foliage; covers itself with daffodil yellow blossoms when in bloom; and flowers earlier than anything else in the garden. Surely such a shrub belongs in any home landscape."

ROSE CLASSES AND CLASSIFICATION

Botanists have organized wild roses into separate species according to genetic differences and the differences in physical characteristics they create. Because they usually descend from a mix of species and cultivars, garden roses do not lend themselves to such a neat categorization. The exact bloodlines of most garden roses are impossible to establish, since until the 20th century few nurserymen kept detailed records of the crosses they made to create the roses they sold.

Still, it is usually possible for experienced rosarians to discern which roses share common parents from physical similarities. Using a combination of visual inspection and reference to existing records of rose-breeding programs, rosarians have organized the cultivated roses into more than a dozen family groups, or "classes." The class of Gallica roses, for example, comprises cultivars believed to be descended directly from *R. gallica* and that share obvious physical similarities (see the description on page 53).

What follows is a brief description of the rose classes best adapted to cultivation in the northern half of the United States—the roses with which Mike Ruggiero has firsthand experience but gardeners elsewhere may also benefit from his knowledge. Those with a long-standing interest in roses may recognize the names of the classes, and the names of some of the cultivars, but even so, they will find much useful information about how these plants will adapt to their gardens and what their strengths are. This, unfortunately, is data often overlooked. For as roses were abandoned by mainstream gardeners, they have increasingly come to be the hobby of specialists, who treat them as collectibles rather than garden plants. For collectors, the mere fact that a plant survives in their garden marks success; gardeners, however, want plants that perform well—reliable roses. In their search for such plants, a familiarity with the adaptations of the different classes will save expensive and time-consuming trial and error.

One last word of explanation: The cultivar names included between brackets at the end of each class description are those of roses that may be found in the Peggy Rockefeller Rose Garden.

OLD GARDEN ROSES

ALBA ROSES

Roses of classes that originated before the emergence of the first Hybrid Tea rose in 1867 are called old garden roses. An individual old garden rose may have been introduced after that date: 'Variegata di Bologna' was introduced in 1909, but this is an authentic old garden rose, because it belongs to the Bourbon class.

Classes of old garden roses vary dramatically in the size and form of their plant and the flowers. Blossoms range from small rosettes of five petals to giant, multipetaled puffs 6 inches or more across. Most are deliciously fragrant, and many are exceptionally cold-hardy. The old garden roses that flourish in the northern half of the country produce most of their blossoms in a single, prolonged flush in late spring or early summer. The blossoms of these plants range in color from white through pink to deep red and purple; yellows are virtually unknown from zone 7 north.

The Albas are robust, winter-hardy shrubs that flourish even on challenging sites. They tend to grow quite large, forming rounded shrubs 6 feet or more tall and broad. In the New York City area they bloom in mid- to late June, bearing flattened, double flowers of modest size (2–3 inches wide) that may range in hue from white to deep pink; the white blossoms commonly possess a particularly strong perfume.

The parentage of the Albas is something of a mystery. The foliage and fruit stems resemble a more refined *R. canina,* a wild hedgerow plant of northern Europe; rosarians speculate that the other parent is *R. gallica* or *R. × damascena.* According to historical sources, a few varieties of Albas were cultivated as early as the Middle Ages, and by 1840 there were 42 distinct cultivars being grown and marketed.

[*Rosa × alba* (white rose of York); 'Celestial'; 'Königin von Dänemark'; 'Maiden's Blush']

BOURBON ROSES

CENTIFOLIA ROSES

This class of roses originated in a wild hedge discovered about 1817 on the Île de Bourbon, in the Indian Ocean, apparently a natural cross of an ever-blooming Chinese rose with a Damask rose, perhaps 'Quatre Saisons'. Bourbon roses combine moderate cold hardiness with lush flowers and a reblooming habit.

Not surprisingly, Bourbons fall into two types. One form resembles their China rose ancestor, with its almost thornless, flexible canes, and the other favors the Damasks, with their thorny, stiffer growth. The flowers range in form from cup-shaped to globular and in color from white to deep pink, scarlet, and cerise. Bourbon roses bloom heavily in early summer and then intermittently throughout the growing season.

['Honorine de Brabant'; 'Louise Odier'; 'Madame Ernst Calvat'; 'Madame Isaac Pereire'; 'Madame Pierre Oger'; 'Variegata di Bologna'; 'Zéphirine Drouhin']

"Cabbage rose" is a popular name for Centifolia roses, and it aptly describes their large and petal-packed blossoms. Members of this class commonly develop into large, somewhat sprawling shrubs. The flowers, which are borne in one flush in late spring or early summer, are usually fragrant, and they droop down from the arching branches. The foliage is typically coarse and dark green, and the canes are generally very thorny.

Although its origins are unknown, this class of roses seems to have sprung from a complicated mix of native European and Middle Eastern species, including *R. gallica* and *R.* × *damascena*. This class was a favorite of post-medieval Europe—more than 200 varieties of Centifolias appeared between 1580 and 1710, and they are often seen in the paintings of the Dutch Old Masters.

['Fantin Latour'; 'Petite de Hollande']

DAMASK ROSES

GALLICA ROSES

The foliage of Damask roses is characteristically gray-green and downy, giving this rose a soft-textured look. Damask shoots are always thorny, with flowers appearing on short, flexible stalks. The flowers themselves are usually modest (commonly 3–4 inches across) and form flattened rosettes of many petals. They are famous for their fragrance. In color they range from white through pastel and pinks to bright red. Most Damasks bear their flowers in a single flush at the beginning of the summer.

Damask roses descend from a Near Eastern species, *R. × damascena*. Damasks are believed to have been cultivated by the ancient Romans, to have disappeared from European gardens with the fall of the Roman Empire, and reintroduced from the Middle East in the 12th or 13th century.

['Celsiana'; 'Ispahan'; 'Madame Hardy'; 'Marie Louise'; 'Quatre Saisons'; 'Trigintipetala' ('Kazanlik')]

Gallicas usually reach about 4 feet in height, flower in early summer, and require little care, tolerating the poorest of soils. They are also notably cold-hardy and tend to be disease-resistant. The foliage is mostly darkish green and has few thorns.

This is one of the ancient rose classes of Europe, a group that appears in ancient Roman wall paintings and in the margins of medieval illuminated manuscripts. The majority of the Gallicas date from the early 19th century, when they were a favorite of the French nurserymen.

['Agathe Incarnata'; 'Belle Isis'; 'Camaieux'; 'Cardinal de Richelieu'; 'Charles de Mills'; 'Complicata'; 'Duchese d'Angoulême'; 'Versicolor' ('Rosa Mundi'); 'Superb Tuscan' ('Tuscany Superb')]

HYBRID MUSK ROSES

HYBRID PERPETUAL ROSES

Although they are a creation of the early 20th century, the Hybrid Musk roses are commonly included with the old garden roses because of the similarity of their flowers in form, fragrance, and blooming season.

Hybrid Musk roses generally make vigorous shrubby plants 4 to 6 feet tall—a few cultivars, such as 'Cornelia', may be tied to a trellis and used as a moderate-size climber. The blossoms are borne on long branches, rebloom reliably if unevenly throughout the growing season, and are heavily scented. The flower colors include a number of delicate and very attractive pinks and apricots as well as some whites and strong reds. Hybrid Musks make excellent specimen plants, landscape shrubs, and ornamental hedges.

['Ballerina'; 'Belinda'; 'Bishop Darlington'; 'Bonn'; 'Buff Beauty'; 'Cornelia'; 'Danaë'; 'Daybreak'; 'Erfurt'; 'Felicia'; 'Lavender Lassie'; 'Penelope'; 'Prosperity'; 'Skyrocket' ('Wilhelm')]

This class resulted from a crossing of Bourbon roses with roses of virtually every other existing class. The first ones appeared in France in the 1840s, and because they rebloomed more freely than the other roses of that era, they were an immediate success.

Hybrid Perpetuals are a varied group, but they commonly make medium-size, moderately vigorous shrubs that bloom heavily in early summer and in smaller flushes into fall. The blossoms range from pure white through pink to crimson, and they tend to be large and full, often reminiscent of a full-blown Hybrid Tea rose in form. Climbing cultivars require ample space; bush types may be espaliered (trained against a wall); Hybrid Perpetual are only moderately cold-hardy and tend to succumb to foliar diseases.

['Alfred Colomb'; 'Baron Girod de l'Ain'; 'Mabel Morrison'; 'Mrs. John Laing'; 'Paul Neyron'; 'Reine des Violettes']

MOSS ROSES

PORTLAND ROSES

The name of this class refers to the curious balsamic-scented glands that cover the flower buds, which indeed look like moss. Moss roses bear highly scented flowers that may take the form of tightly constructed saucers of petals or rather loosely packed puffs. The canes are often unusually well armed with thorns. All of the Mosses bloom heavily in early summer; some rebloom sparingly later in the season.

The first Moss rose seems to have appeared as a spontaneous mutation (a "sport") on a branch of a Centifolia rose sometime prior to the mid-18th century. Highly popular in their day, the Moss roses have an antique charm that has made them nostalgic favorites.

['Alfred de Dalmas'; 'Capitaine John Ingram'; 'Chapeau de Napoléon'; 'Deuil de Paul Fontaine'; 'Gloire des Mousseux'; 'Henri Martin'; 'Little Gem'; 'Madame de la Roche-Lambert'; 'Madame Louis Lévêque'; 'Mrs. William Paul']

This class originated with a bush found in Italy during the 18th century by the Duchess of Portland. It was hailed as a great discovery because after the first early-summer flush of blossoms, Portland roses will rebloom, though only occasionally. Portland roses are among the best old roses for a small garden, however, because of their hardiness and their size: they tend to form compact shrubs 3 to 4 feet tall and broad. The flowers are typically of medium size (3 to 4 inches in diameter), very fragrant, and pink to red in color.

['Comte de Chambord'; 'Jacques Cartier' ('Marchesa Boccella'); 'Rose du Roi']

Rosa Centifolia.   *Rosier à cent feuilles.*

P. J. Redouté.   Langlois.

2

ROSES THAT
ARE RIGHT FOR
YOUR GARDEN

V isitors to the Peggy Rockefeller Rose Garden are selecting roses for their own gardens, so they always ask Mike Ruggiero the same question: "What is the best rose?" And he always gives the same replay: "That depends." Then he adds: "One of my favorite roses ever was 'Sheer Bliss'." This Hybrid Tea is renowned for its palest pink flowers that shade at their hearts to a deeper blush; the flowers are fragrant, too. It was his favorite "until I tried to grow it. Try to get that one through a New York winter."

What's his point? "If you can't grow it, it can't be your favorite."

Novices may overlook this point through lack of experience—and yet experienced gardeners often ignore it, too, determined to overcome nature through horticultural tricks. But as experienced rosarians like Mike Ruggiero know, the only successful long-term rose garden begins with an analysis of the site: light, water, and soil conditions. Roses with preferences for the conditions in your yard are the ones you should consider growing. That may seem self-evident, but the steps that Ruggiero follows in this process differ somewhat from those the gardener might use in selecting from other groups of plants.

He is adamant about not choosing roses for the gardeners he meets in the Peggy Rockefeller Rose Garden, because the visitors are as varied as the roses. When asked to name the best, he first interviews these gardeners. What color of roses do they prefer? Do they want fragrant flowers? Do they favor the delicacy of small flowers or the impact of large ones? Then he asks about the conditions in their garden: its exposure to sun and wind, the composition of its soil, and the space it will allow for roses—can it absorb an expansive bush? Finally, he asks them about their level of commitment to this project: Are they willing to invest some extra work in growing a rose cultivar that may be beautiful but also less carefree. Once he has assembled all this information, he offers a list of five or six different roses that fit the profile.

> *I try never to make the choice for them, but rather say, "This is what you can grow." Some people actually don't care about fragrance.*

"I try never to make the choice for them, but rather say, 'This is what you can grow.'" What people like or dislike sometimes surprises this seasoned rosarian. "Some people actually don't care about fragrance. I'm shocked."

Assessing rose suitability. Because of their diverse parentage (depending on the type of rose, it may descend from Asian, European, or even North American natives), roses vary widely in their adaptation to climate and soil. *R. rugosa* (an Asian species), for example, thrives in dry, sandy soils and areas with intense winter cold, whereas Tea roses (which descend from roses of subtropical southern China) thrive in the subtropical heat and humidity of the Deep South. Identifying the classes of roses suitable for their garden is the very first decision would-be rose growers should make.

At NYBG, for example, you will find no Tea roses, because as a class, the Tea roses are not winter-hardy in the New York metropolitan area. Portland roses, on the other hand, have not only proved reliably winter-hardy at NYBG, they overwinter successfully there without the protection given to other classes such as Hybrid Teas. Hybrid Perpetual roses, by contrast, may offer many fine shrubs and are outstanding sources of cut flowers, but they are not suited to the New York climate. Because they are descended largely from Tea roses, Hybrid Perpetuals are marginally winter-hardy at NYBG. Compounding this liability is the fact that they have a special susceptibility to blackspot, a fungal disease that flourishes in New York City's hot, humid summers. Blackspot causes afflicted Hybrid Perpetuals to shed their leaves, and although a bush may grow a new crop of foliage by fall, the disease so weakens it that it enters the winter less able to withstand the cold. When Ruggiero wanted to make room in the rose garden for the new David Austin English roses, the Hybrid Perpetuals were the first to go.

A lesser-known class that he recommends highly to home gardeners is the Hybrid Musks. This is an old-fashioned class now rarely seen in home gardens, which is a pity, since Hybrid Musks are winter-hardy and disease-resistant, and they rebloom well after producing their first flush of flowers in early summer. Individual blossoms are smaller than those of a Hybrid Tea—often far smaller, as in the case of the Hybrid Musk 'Belinda', whose flowers (pink with a white eye at the center) measure just ¾ inch across. Yet so heavily does 'Belinda' bloom that when in full flower it is one of the favorites of all who see it in the Peggy Rockefeller Rose Garden. 'Ballerina', another Hybrid Musk, is also a favorite: its flowers look like a paler and simpler version of those borne by 'Belinda'; whereas the latter's blossoms are double (many-petaled), those of 'Ballerina' are single (that is, they include just one round of five petals).

Rose classes for particular climates. Choosing a class of roses that suits the climate of your region is the first step in planning a successful planting. (A guide to rose classes and climates appears on pages 51 to 55.) But it is also essential to analyze the particular growing conditions of your own garden. For even though roses are a diverse group, they share certain fundamental needs. In general, roses need well-drained soil and a sunny site, and gardeners who want to plant roses should try to locate a spot within their landscape that supplies those basic requirements. A garden that offers only partial shade and perpetually damp soil requires special choices of rose classes and cultivars.

The ideal spot for a rose garden is both airy and flat and receives 7 to 8 hours of sun daily, and you must have all these things, as well as a good loam soil if you are to grow Hybrid Tea roses successfully. But excellent drainage is the most essential point, for, as Mike Ruggiero points out, "You can improve the soil, but changing the drainage is a major undertaking."

Drainage issues. A simple drainage test that he recommends all gardeners perform is to dig a hole, place in it a pot with drainage holes in the bottom, and fill it with water. If the water drains away within a few minutes, that is a sign that your soil is probably excessively sandy and will need improvement with lots of organic material—sphagnum peat or compost—for any roses except the Rugosas. If the

Winter-hardy and disease-resistant, Hybrid Musk roses ('Belinda', ABOVE, and 'Ballerina', OPPOSITE) are an old-fashioned class that flowers successfully in sunny home gardens.

water takes an hour or two to drain away, drainage is only average, but still adequate for growing roses. Beyond 2 hours, roses simply will not thrive. To Ruggiero's knowledge, only one rose will survive a poorly drained soil, and remarkably the same rose also tolerates shade: the aptly named swamp rose, *R. palustris,* a little-known native of eastern North America that is available from a few mail-order nurseries. A 6-foot-tall shrub that sends up suckers from its roots and will spread into a thicket if unchecked, *R. palustris* is hardly the plant for a formal setting. Still, it bears pretty, bright pink flowers and the foliage turns golden in fall; although probably not the best choice for a specimen plant in a small urban garden, it is an excellent shrub for an informal setting such as the edge of a meadow.

Ruggiero learned the importance of drainage from firsthand experience, for the NYBG rose garden that preceded the present one had problems with wet soil, and the roses there, even though they got plenty of sun, tended to be short-lived. When the Peggy Rockefeller Rose Garden was being installed, he helped to install an extensive system of drainage pipes (called "tile") under the site. Then he worked with a contractor to create an ideal soil mix. This soil was mixed off-site and delivered in a truck, but Ruggiero and the contractor brought it into the garden in wheelbarrows so as not to damage the drainage pipes below; ultimately, the rose beds were filled with this special mix to a depth of 2 feet.

You can improve the soil, but changing the drainage would be a major undertaking.

Obviously, few home gardeners would go to this extreme, but Ruggiero says NYBG was vindicated when an 8-inch water main that ran through the garden ruptured and flooded the rose beds. Yet within hours of when the main was capped, all the excess water had drained away.

Solving problems with poor drainage. There are alternatives to laying tile for solving drainage problems. One is to improve the soil with a crumbs, through which water can drain. This technique, while valuable for plantings of a few roses, is impractical for larger plantings, since amending a large bed might involve bringing in a truckload of compost. In such a case, the gardener might consider creating a raised bed, either by filling in a frame made of timber or stone, or by just mounding soil in the bed to a level several inches higher than the surrounding area. Of course, the gardener could also choose to cultivate Miniature roses in pots or other containers.

Hazards of exposure to cold. Growing roses in raised beds or containers does, however, require some special care. When roses are raised up out of the ground, their root systems are more exposed to the cold—the chill can penetrate from the sides as well as from the top. It is essential then to select roses that are not too vigorous, those that will not rapidly fill the soil with roots right to the wall of the pot; the roots will need a jacket of soil to act as insulation and help protect them from freezing, thawing, and then refreezing with every change in the weather. This precaution is especially important in a terrace garden, which is even more exposed to the weather. Miniature roses (many of which are quite cold-hardy), not some expansive shrub such as 'New Dawn', are the class of choice for a terrace on a high-rise apartment building.

In addition, grafted roses, those that have been propagated by grafting, as the bulk of commerical roses are, when grown in raised beds and containers benefit from planting with the graft union (the swollen point where the canes join the rootstock) slightly below the surface of the soil. The graft union is also vulnerable to cold, and in an exposed situation it needs the protection of a blanket of soil.

Testing garden soil. For assessing a site's soil, nothing can equal having a comprehensive soil test performed on samples taken from your proposed planting areas. Such a test can be arranged through your local Cooperative Extension Service office (found under the county or state office listings in the blue pages of the telephone book) and typically costs $10 or less. It offers a detailed analysis of soil texture and organic content, which in turn will guide you as to the soil's water-holding capacity and its permeability; that is, its ability to absorb and retain water. A complete soil test also reveals the soil's nutrient-holding capacity as well as indicating how easily roots will spread through it.

Getting an assessment of the soil's organic content is particularly important. Most gardeners, when they do perform a soil test, test only for the three major elements: nitrogen (chemical symbol N), phosphorous (P), and potassium (K). However, while the NPK test will help indicate fertilizer requirements, it won't reveal the organic makeup of your soil. Knowing this before you plant is essential, because roses are "greedy feeders." They take large amounts of nutrients from the soil and need the extra fertility of a soil rich in organic matter.

If your soil would benefit from the addition of more humus, more compost, leaf mold, or sphagnum peat, then the time to add this is before putting in the plants. "The hardest thing to do is to change the structure of the soil once a plant is in," Mike Ruggiero explains. "Sure, you can build up the top periodically [by mulching with organic materials], but you can't build the bottom after the plants are established."

When having your soil tested, it is crucial to furnish the soil-testing lab with separate samples from each area you intend to plant. Providing the lab with one sample, a mixture of soil taken from different areas, may save a few dollars, but the profile will not be as accurate. Dog owners should not take a sample from an area where pets urinate, as the sample will not yield valid test results. Finally, since the Cooperative Extension office will probably supply an addressed box and instruct you to mail your samples to the testing lab, remember that a dry sample weighs less, and so requires less postage, than a soggy one.

Testing soil mixes. Because he makes a point of practicing what he preaches, Ruggiero tested sample after sample when developing the soil mix for the Peggy Rockefeller Rose Garden. "[The contractor] would bring me a 5-gallon-bucket sample every other day and I'd say 'not enough organic.' " When the mix finally passed his rigid standards, it consisted of approximately 60 percent topsoil (sandy topsoil or loam), 30 percent leaf compost, and 10 percent peat. The peat, he explains, holds a bit of water but never really breaks down, while the leaf compost eventually breaks down and disappears. The resulting mixture amounts to a soil that is well drained but holds a little bit of water—which is exactly what you want. As Ruggiero puts it, "Roses hate water, but they love water."

How deep should this improved, well-drained soil be? At least 8 to 10 inches to accommodate a full-size shrub rose. Better yet is a soil depth of 16 to 24 inches. In some areas of the NYBG rose garden, the soil runs as deep as 30 inches. This sounds extreme, but in fact a rose's need in this respect is about the same as that of peonies or irises.

Light requirements. After soil and drainage, the amount of sunlight a garden gets is probably the most crucial factor when determining what types of roses will do well. Although some roses may succeed in a semishaded spot, an area that receives an average of 4 to 5 hours of direct sunlight daily will support a far greater range. A bit of shade at the right time, however, is helpful: if your roses are shaded from 1:00 to 4:00 in the afternoon, the hottest part of the day, the blossoms will stay

"Blue veil" is the direct translation of 'Veilchenblau', a Hybrid Multiflora rose that prefers the kind of shady site most roses will not tolerate and bears just one flush of violet-colored flowers each summer.

fresh longer and won't lose their colors as quickly. Protection of this kind is especially valuable in hot-weather areas such as the Deep South.

What are the shade-tolerant roses? 'Veilchenblau', an old rambler that blooms once a summer and whose name means "blue veil" in German, actually performs better in a shaded site. The clusters of small blossoms have a better color in such a location; direct sun bleaches them from violet to an unattractive purplish pink. This rose is descended from the Asian species *R. multiflora,* the living fence that has become such a weed in North America; *R. multiflora* thrives even in the middle of the woods, and Ruggiero suggests that those with shady gardens look to its descendants for their roses. Besides 'Veilchenblau', there is the thornless rambler 'Tausendschon', whose clusters include blossoms from deep pink to white, and 'Violette', which resembles 'Veilchenblau', except that the flowers are a deeper violet in hue.

Heat and humidity. After these factors, gardeners need to consider the host of local conditions that are usually lumped together under the heading of "exposure." A hot, dry site such as the front yard of a beach cottage makes Rugosa roses and the hybrids bred from them a good choice. These roses thrive in conditions of arid, sandy soil; wind; and

Individual blossoms of 'Trier', ABOVE, and in mass, OPPOSITE, open wide to collect sun. The Hybrid Multiflora rose flourishes in hot, dry seaside conditions.

Rosa
'Dortmund'
Kordesii rose

even salt spray. Two of Ruggiero's favorites for a hot, dry site are the Hybrid Rugosa rose *R. rugosa* 'Rubra' and a multiflora-descended shrub with creamy white blossoms, 'Trier'.

Hot and humid conditions, such as those found in a low-lying south- or west-facing garden enclosed by hedges or trees, dictate a very different selection of roses. Blackspot flourishes in such a spot, and any roses planted there must be strongly disease-resistant, especially if the gardener is reluctant to maintain a schedule of fungicidal sprays. Ruggiero recommends as particularly resistant the shrubs and climbers bred in Germany from *R. kordesii:* 'Dortmund', which bears single red flowers with a white eye; 'Hamburger Phoenix', which has dark crimson blossoms; and 'Leverkusen', which blooms a lemon yellow. In addition, he has never observed blackspot on the pink-flowered Modern Shrub rose 'Carefree Wonder', the mauve-flowered Floribunda

Equally handsome if espaliering on a fence, OPPOSITE, or sprawling informally in a garden, ABOVE, 'Dortmund' thrives in the heat and humidity that often troubles many other roses.

'Escapade', or the white-flowered Hybrid Tea 'Jardins de Bagatelle'.

Winter conditions. The opposite climatic conditions—winter cold and winter winds can also pose a challenge, and not just in the far north. A garden in what is normally a temperate zone may suffer the same stresses if it is located at high altitude, or even just on an exposed northern slope where the roses are battered by every storm that crosses the Canadian border or the Rockies. For gardeners in this situation, Ruggiero recommends the new Canadian Explorer Series of roses. These were bred specifically for cold hardiness, and they have proved outstandingly reliable in the Peggy Rockefeller Rose Garden. One rose of this series, a shrub named 'William Baffin' that bears deep pink blossoms with yellow centers, is planted at the top of the grand stone staircase down to the rose garden. Despite the location in this "wind tunnel," 'William Baffin' has overwintered there without damage and without special protection. For cold, exposed sites Ruggiero also recommends the Kordesii roses, which are as resistant to cold as to humidity and which also overwinter successfully at NYBG without protection.

How the rose will be used. Environmental factors and personal taste aren't the only elements that should influence the selection process. The use of the rose in the landscape—as an accent, a hedge, or a backdrop in a border—also determines which rose is best. Obviously, if you intend to train the rose up a wall or along a fence, then climbing roses or ramblers are more appropriate. For a group planting Hybrid Teas and Floribundas look impressive, but they don't work well as single plants—the flowers are glorious, but the shrubs are somewhat twiggy

On a cold, windy, north-facing site, few roses grow as successfully as 'William Baffin', a Canadian Shrub that is grown as a climber at NYBG.

and ungainly. A shrub rose is a better option for working just a single bush into an existing garden. These bushes have a more rounded form that makes them a better choice for use as a flowering hedge, too.

So if your garden provides the essential sunlight and soil conditions, and if you take the time to explore your garden environment fully, you can be confident of choosing roses that will thrive.

Personal preferences. As for Mike Ruggiero's personal choices, "I love some roses and I dislike others. I don't even like what my wife likes. I love 'Carefree Wonder'. I think it's a great loose rose that just looks like it belongs in a big floppy hedge. And it'll flower its brains out for you. I love roses like 'Pink Peace' because of its hot smell. I like 'Betty Prior', which has been around since dirt. But I don't like any rose that we're constantly spraying because of blackspot. And I don't like any rose that's not winter-hardy. Choosing roses, it's personal . . . and that's what makes the world nice, you know."

From the famous German rose nurseryman, Reimer Kordes, the Floribunda rose 'Lilli Marleen' is colorful as a group planting in a featured bed of the Peggy Rockefeller Rose Garden.

Southeast: Southern gardeners struggled for years, trying to grow Hybrid Tea, Grandiflora, and Floribunda roses in a climate that is too hot and humid for those modern hybrids. Dr. William Welch, an Extension Landscape Specialist, has explored the roses that flourished in southern gardens before the creation of Hybrid Teas and before the invention of fungicides (see *Antique Roses for the South*, Taylor Publishing Company, 1990).

With each of the clases he recommends below, Dr. Welch has also included representative cultivars that are personal favorites.

1. China roses: Repeat-blooming drought-tolerant shrubs, typically with a compact, rounded form. Not hardy in the North. ['Old Blush'; 'Cramoisi Supérieur'; 'Archduke Charles']

2. Tea roses: Repeat-blooming, commonly bearing large, very double, nodding flowers. Not hardy in the North. ['Mrs. B.R. Cant'; 'Mrs. Dudley Cross']

3. Noisettes: A class first bred in South Carolina in the 19th century. Noisettes typically bear medium-size, double flowers in clusters and are repeat-blooming. Most are vigorous climbers. ['Jaune Desprez'; 'Blush Noisette'; 'Madame Albert Carriére']

4. Polyanthas: Ancestors of the Floribundas, Polyantha roses bear small, double flowers in clusters on dwarf, shapely shrubs. ['Cécile Brünner'; 'Marie Pavié'; 'La Marne']

5. Species and species hybrids [*R. banksiae lutea* and *alba plena;* 'Fortuniana'; *R. palustris; R. multiflora* 'Carnea']

6. Hybrid Perpetuals ['Paul Neyron'; climbing 'American Beauty']

7. Bourbons ['Souvenir de la Malmaison'; 'Zéphirine Drouhin']

8. Hybrid Musks ['Trier'; 'Penelope'; 'Felicia']

Northern New England: For ten years Suzanne Verrier operated Forevergreen Farm in North Yarmouth, Maine, a legend among North Country rose gardeners.

"In Maine," she explains, "you have two very different areas: inland and coastal. You can have a warm zone 5 or a cold zone 6, so many rose classes are a 'mixed bag,' with some cultivars within the class doing better than others. 'Dr. W. Van Fleet' [a large-flowered climber] you'll have trouble growing inland, but it does great on the coast."

In general, Verrier recommends the following classes for northern New England (Vermont, New Hampshire, northern Massachusetts, and northern Connecticut). (See also her *Rosa Rugosa,* Capability Books, 1991 and *Gallica Roses,* 1996.)

1. Gallica roses

2. Alba roses

3. Centifolia roses

4. Damask roses

5. Bourbon roses
(the hardier cultivars)

6. Musk roses (the hardier cultivars)

7. Rugosa roses: "The new German 'Pavement Series' are great in borders."

8. David Austin's English roses "do brilliantly." ['The Herbalist'; 'Abraham Darby'; 'Charmian']

9. Griffith Buck roses: "Incredible here." These are Modern Shrub roses bred for winter hardiness and disease resistance by Dr. Griffith Buck of Iowa State University. ['Amiga Mia'; 'Carefree Beauty'; 'Country Dancer']

Rocky Mountain West: High Country Rosarium in Denver, Colorado, is one of the most respected rose nurseries in the high country, and it is a particularly rich source of regionally adapted roses. Heather Cambell operates the nursery with her father, Bill Cambell.

Roses that perform well in dry climates at high elevations include:

1. *Rugosa roses*
2. *Alba roses*
3. *Gallica roses*
4. *Damask roses*
5. *Species roses:* Many species roses flourish in the mountain west; *R. glauca* in particular (and it does not defoliate as it does in New York).
6. *Modern Shrub roses/climbers* ['Dortmund'; 'Golden Wings'; 'New Dawn']
7. *Miniatures:* These have proved very hardy, in part because they are commonly propagated as own-root roses. High Country Rosarium grows all its roses on their own roots, rather than on a standard rootstock (see chapter 4, page 104, for explanation).

Pacific Coast: As curator of the rose collection at the Huntington Botanical Gardens in San Marino, California, Clair Martin III presides over what is arguably the choicest selection of roses, old and new, in North America. Because of the immense geographical range of California, every class of rose can be grown in that state. He prefers to specify what won't grow in certain regions.

In the desert/southwest area, for example, rose classes such as the Gallicas and Rugosas that thrive in cold climates do not perform well. Alba roses do well in the warmer parts of this region. In general, the cold-hardy rose classes perform better from Santa Barbara northward, and up into the mountains. David Austin's English roses thrive, but they may outgrow the average garden since they commonly reach a height and spread of 10 to 12 feet.

Upper Midwest: As a plant breeder in the Woody Ornamental Research Project at the Minnesota Landscape Arboretum, Kathy Zuzek is actively involved in finding roses that flourish in a region where winter temperatures commonly drop to −30°F. Growing roses in Minnesota, according to Zuzek, is "like growing herbaceous perennials" in milder regions; the challenge is to find a rose that doesn't die back to the crown every winter.

The following are the rose classes that Zuzek recommends:

1. *Alba roses*
2. *Damask roses*
3. *Gallica roses:* Because these bushes are compact, more of their canes are shielded by snow cover, and they tend to suffer less winterkill.
4. *Rugosa roses:* Reliably hardy, the species Rugosas and their hybrids offer the best reblooming roses for this region.
5. *Floribundas:* Some cultivars, such as 'Nearly Wild', have proved reasonably hardy.
6. *Griffith Buck roses:* Dr. Buck's widow has donated his collection of roses and his breeding stock to the Minnesota Landscape Arboretum. Buck's legacy includes such outstandingly hardy shrubs as the semidouble pink-flowered rose 'Amiga Mia' and the orange-pink 'Prairie Princess'.

3

DESIGNING
WITH ROSES

ike Ruggiero is the first to admit that he is not a garden designer. He never had to create a plan for the rose garden he cultivates—he inherited a plan from one of America's greatest designers. But in his years as senior curator, he has had to adjust the Peggy Rockefeller Rose Garden's planting plan. He is constantly finding space for new rosebushes, and he is periodically faced with the task of replacing plantings that simply haven't worked out. What he has gathered from this experience is the conviction that practical design—deciding where to put what rose, and divining how each cultivar is best displayed—comes down to common sense.

This commonsense style of design is especially relevant today because of the changes that are taking place in rose gardening. For most American gardeners, the image that comes to mind when we think of a rose planting is of a formal design such as that found in the NYBG garden. This type of garden—one in which orderly row after row of roses dominate to the exclusion of nearly all other plants—is the product of a centuries-old tradition. Certainly it offers a most impressive setting for the display of rose blossoms. It also affords a practical response to conventional bedding roses such as Hybrid Teas, which must be sprayed on a schedule and pruned, fertilized, and winter-protected according to a single method, operations far easier to carry out if the roses are grouped together.

But a traditional rose garden of this sort has little appeal for most modern gardeners. How many of us have either the space or the resources to mount such a display? Fortunately, the reappearance of healthy roses, which do not demand such a rigid, specialized kind of maintenance, has made these plants far easier to integrate into the garden at large. So, after a couple of centuries of seclusion, roses are

ABOVE: Climbing and Shrub roses mix easily with perennials and container plantings around a poolside cabana. OPPOSITE: Rosebushes intermingle with perennial and annual flowers in a mixed border.

moving back out into the flower garden, the mixed border, and the herb garden, and they are even finding use as landscape shrubs.

As the roses make this move, pragmatic design becomes more and more important. Planting a formal rose garden may involve reams of architectural renderings and complicated plant combinations. Finding a spot in the garden for a favorite rose—or perhaps for a few favorite roses—is a far simpler, more rule-of-thumb process.

CHOOSING A SITE

Having decided to install a few—or perhaps many—rosebushes in your garden, how do you choose the best spots? And how do you arrange the roses there? Planning a successful rose garden involves a balancing act: you must take care to coordinate your needs with those of the roses.

The design you create should suit your tastes, of course, and fit the site. But it must also provide the comforts that a rose demands, if your bushes are to be reliable performers.

Setting priorities. Ruggiero puts the needs of the plants first, since roses cannot compromise. Choose a site that is sunny, he advises—and in a cool-climate area, the sunnier the better. Make sure it is breezy, as good air circulation in the summertime reduces the incidence of fungal diseases. (He believes this is why roses perform so well on the eastern end of Long Island, New York, because there they are continually swept by less humid breezes

OPPOSITE: Single and double roses intertwine with herbaceous flowers, forming a living bouquet in a rose collector's garden in Richmond, Virginia. ABOVE: Daisies and roses pair in a simple yet irresistible display.

coming in off the ocean.) Above all, though, in locating a rose plant-ing, make sure that you don't choose a low-lying "frost pocket" where water and cold air collect.

INTEGRATING ROSES INTO THE GARDEN

If roses are to be nestled in among perennials, annuals, and shrubs, then, as noted earlier, the Hybrid Teas and Floribundas are poor choices. They integrate poorly with other types of plants. Far better for a situation of this kind are the old garden roses, which with their arch-ing canes and shrublike form have a far more graceful profile. Plant-ing old garden roses involves a bit of sacrifice, since they do not repeat

ABOVE: A compact Polyantha rose 'Mrs. R. M. Finch' punctuates a bed of irises, foxgloves, and snapdragons. OPPOSITE: The Gallica 'La Belle Sultane' flowers amid an expanse of chives.

their blossoming as regularly and freely as modern everblooming roses do. But that does not mean they are shy bloomers; during their season the old garden roses smother themselves with blossoms. Ruggiero suggests that instead of comparing these plants with modern everblooming roses, you treat old garden roses as another kind of hardy, seasonal shrub such as a lilac, hydrangea, weigela, or azalea.

Integrating everbloomers. If the everblooming habit is essential and the rose must still mingle with other plants, then he recommends David Austin English roses, which repeat-bloom like modern roses but which have kept some of the growth habits of the more

ABOVE: David Austin's English rose 'Evelyn' boasts antique rose fragrance and charm with modern everblooming habit. OPPOSITE: English Rose 'Constance Spry' provides soft visual counterpoint to Clematis jackmanii.

graceful old-timers. Modern Shrub roses, of course, are another alternative, since these frequently combine a compact, mounded form of growth with repeat-blooming flowers.

ROSES IN A FORMAL SETTING

If a formal garden design better suits your yard and your house, there are several ways to incorporate roses. One of the most effective uses of roses in the formal garden is as "standards" or "tree roses," which are really simple forms of topiary. Rose standards usually consist of a Hybrid Tea rose that has been grafted onto the top of a long, upright trunk of some rootstock rose; the Hybrid Tea is pruned into a more or less spherical form, so that the result somewhat resembles a small tree. This has an artificial look that may seem out of place in a naturalistic garden, but standards' architectural form works beautifully in a formal setting.

The Hybrid Tea rose 'First Prize' performs beautifully as a standard rose tree in the Peggy Rockefeller Rose Garden. Mike Ruggiero recommends these rose topiaries for formal settings and period gardens.

Rose standards. "It's very Victorian," Ruggiero explains; rose standards are perfect for giving a garden a period feel. "They're great for use in entranceways to the garden, or on each side of a gate or a path, or as a focal point in the garden. Standards are also great for people with bad backs because you don't have to bend down to smell them."

Rose standards may planted in the ground, but they look especially fine when planted in ornate pots. Be forewarned, though, that rose standards require extra work to bring them through the winter alive. The fact that the flower-bearing hybrid bush is borne atop a long stem makes them especially vulnerable to frost-damage—if the trunk is damaged anywhere, then the hybrid top dies, and with it the ability to bear the desirable hybrid flowers. So whereas ordinary bush Hybrid Teas usually need no more protection than some soil hilled up around their bases, standards must be dug out of the ground ("lifted") in late fall and then either replanted in tubs and moved to a frost-free garage, or laid down on the round and buried with soil.

Container roses. Potted roses can make splendid ornaments for almost any garden, and they are particularly effective in a formal setting. But if you choose to grow roses in pots, plant cultivars that are comfortable with this kind of restriction. An obvious choice is the Miniature roses: their diminutive top growth is matched by a comparably small root system, so they won't feel crowded when planted into a tub or large pot.

Planting roses in containers allows tremendous flexibility in the matter of design. It is, after all, a relatively simple matter to move a tub or large pot, so you can shift your roses around until you find just the placement you like. You'll pay for this flexibility, however, with some extra maintenance: container roses need regular irrigation, and consequently more generous fertilization to replace the nutrients that the extra water washes away.

Repetition creates a rhythm on this weathered Cape Cod trellis, so that even a commonplace rose such as 'Climbing Blaze' looks unique in its abundance.

Espaliers. There is yet another formal style of rose growing that Ruggiero particularly favors: "I like to espalier them out on a fence." Tying down the rose canes so that they spread outward horizontally causes flowering shoots to spring out from all over the espaliered canes. If the espaliering is done carefully, and canes are tied onto the fence in ascending tiers, the effect can be a solid sheet of flowers.

Espaliering is not only visually effective, in many cases it is also the easiest way to grow a particular cultivar. By raising canes up into the air and separating one from another, it practically guarantees that there will be good air circulation around the foliage, and this will help any cultivar fight off fungal diseases. In addition, some of the more sprawling and thornier cultivars such as the super-vigorous climber 'Silver Moon' may be very difficult to prune or spray when grown as a free-standing bush. Getting into the center of the bush may be nearly impossible. But when tied against a fence, the canes are instantly accessible. Such vigorous roses lend themselves to espaliering, too, because they throw out new canes freely from their bases. If one of the espaliered canes should die, then it is a simple matter to tie a new one in the dead cane's place.

Espaliering is also a practical way to introduce roses into a garden that is too small to accommodate the same plants if cultivated as shrubs. This, in fact, was the origin of the technique: espaliering was invented by the cultivators of small gardens in Europe, gardens where every bit of space was precious. Espaliered plants are not only compact, however; they also add an elegant, almost courtly look to a garden and so are ideal for formal designs.

CLIMBERS AND RAMBLERS

These roses will be of special interest to those gardeners who want to cover up a garden eyesore such as an old tree stump, screen out an unattractive view, or simply add a third dimension (height) to an otherwise flat garden. Climbers and ramblers are most often trained up a trellis or post or over an arbor, but they may also be allowed to scramble across the ground or down over the edge of a wall.

There are hundreds of climbers from which to choose, and as with any other group of roses, selecting the cultivar best adapted to your conditions and your design needs is the best way to ensure horticultural success. Unfortunately, the selection of climbers to be found at the local garden center is particularly poor. Ruggiero believes this is why he sees the same half dozen ramblers and climbers used over and over again, even though they are often not good choices for the situations in which he finds them.

"I see mostly the small 'Blaze' used on gates. And [on walls, fences, and trellises] most people are using the larger climbers like 'New Dawn' or 'Silver Moon', which flower only once. Or they use the Hybrid Teas or the large-flowered climbers that bloom more often but don't do as well in winter. I see 'Don Juan' used even more than 'New Dawn'."

Nearly all the readily available climbing roses—those sold in garden centers and the mass-market catalogs of general seed and nursery stock—are Hybrid Teas. These are not really winter-hardy in the North;

ABOVE: Rosa multiflora *'Carnea' arching over the gate adds some height to an otherwise horizontal display. FOLLOWING PAGE: Rose 'New Dawn' and clematis (Clematis florida Sieboldii) wrap a wooden post.*

in the hard winter of 1993–94, the climbing Hybrid Teas died back all the way to the ground even in the relatively sheltered rose garden at NYBG. For the average home gardener, he would certainly recommend something hardier, such as the Kordesii rose 'Illusion', or one of the roses in the Canadian Explorer Series, such as 'William Baffin'. But to obtain plants of these, you will have to explore the mail-order nurseries that specialize in roses.

If you are determined to grow climbing Hybrid Tea roses in the North, Ruggiero advises that you make sure the site in which you plant them is very well drained. Even so, he recommends releasing all the canes from the trellis or other support once cold weather sets in, laying them down on the ground, and burying them under loose soil until spring. Personally, he isn't sure they are worth that effort when there are so many fine and hardy climbers, such as the Kordesii roses, to be grown (see Climbers and Ramblers, pages 164 to 168).

ROSE HEDGES

Whether your garden plan is formal or informal, roses can furnish materials for a beautiful and functional hedge. A rose hedge provides real security for your property: plant one of the thornier types and no one is going to push their way through it. If a formal effect is desired, you can keep the hedge sheared. 'The Fairy', a compact old Polyantha rose (Polyanthas were ancestors of the Floribundas), is often kept trimmed into a 3-foot-tall hedge. Ruggiero prefers the more informal, freer effect that may be had by planting a landscape rose such as 'Carefree Wonder' or 'Bonica' or one of the more compact Floribundas such as 'Simplicity' or 'Escapade' and letting the bushes develop a more natural shape.

R. rugosa is also a rose that he favors for an informal hedge. For this use he prefers the tough, species-type Rugosas rather than the Hybrid Rugosa cultivars. The pink-flowered variety *R. rugosa* 'Rubra' is a particular favorite. All these nearly wild Rugosas have foliage that is virtually disease-proof and perfumed, reblooming flowers. If allowed to set fruit, they will ornament themselves with fat, colorful hips as well.

OTHER ATTRACTIONS:
FOLIAGE, HIPS, AND THORNS

The glorious flowers are, of course, what sets roses apart from all other shrubs. Still, in our preoccupation with the bloom, we too often lose sight of other important attractions.

For example, roses can be excel as foliage plants. Indeed, the foliage is virtually the only attraction of the central European species, *R. glauca;* this bush bears small and insignificant pink blossoms, but it has rich purplish red leaves. Unfortunately, it has been Ruggiero's experience that no amount of spraying will keep *R. glauca*'s foliage free of fungal diseases, so that by midsummer the specimen in the Peggy Rockefeller Rose Garden is nearly leafless. In a sunny and arid climate such as that of the Rocky Mountain states, he suspects that this rose would perform better.

Hips—the fruits of the rose—add an important element to a shrub's display, as with Rosa glauca, *a specimen of the redleaf rose.*

For the Northeast, however, he prefers the Rugosa roses as foliage plants. He admires these roses' shiny green and rugged foliage: the leaves have a crumpled texture like crepe. In fall the Rugosa foliage turns an attractive yellow, too. And he also likes the delicacy of *R. hugonis* foliage. This Chinese species has fine, almost fernlike leaflets.

The Rugosas are likewise star performers with respect to hips: their fruits are tomato red, round, and ½ an inch in diameter. *R. moyesii*, yet another Chinese species, makes an interesting contrast with its long, slender hips, which are sometimes described as "urn-shaped."

Gardening for rose hips. To raise a really good crop of hips, the gardener will have to adjust maintenance procedures a bit. Normally, deadheading (removing flower heads as they grow old and begin to wilt) is considered an essential part of the rose gardener's routine. Snipping off the aging blooms prevents a bush from setting seed, and preventing it from setting seed ensures that the bush will put all of its energy into bearing more flowers. But since hips are nothing more than seed-bearing fruits, conscientious deadheading will also prevent a bush from bearing hips. If both flowers and hips are wanted, then a compromise must be struck.

Ruggiero suggests that you stop deadheading in September, which will guarantee a long and heavy season of bloom, then let the hips develop as a complement to the fall foliage colors and as a delicious harvest. Continuing to deadhead into the fall will only encourage

Rose foliage often appeals as much as a bloom. Many cultivars, such as Rosa glauca, *boast leaves with attractive reddish tints.*

rosebushes to keep pushing out new growth from the base; such new shoots will not have time to mature sufficiently before the onset of cold weather, and so they will fall victim to winterkill. Better to enjoy your fall hips, and let them help winterize your roses.

Can thorns be anything but a source of grief to the rose gardener? Try a bush of *R. sericea pteracantha,* the wingthorn. This shrub from China is a double oddity. It bears flowers of four petals, whereas virtually every other rose bears petals in multiples of five. But an even more striking distinction is the large and broad, translucent, bloodred thorns that stud the stems. When backlit they glow like rubies.

ROSES AS GROUND COVERS

There is much talk among rosarians of planting roses as a flowering ground cover. Mike Ruggiero has mixed feelings about this. He agrees that some types of roses can make a striking and effective ground cover, but it is a ground cover that is painful and difficult to maintain.

Thorns are the principal problem. How does the gardener weed a ground cover that stabs and grabs? Another problem is the roses' intolerance for foot traffic. Sooner or later the gardener will have to step into the bed of ground cover to replant or prune, or rake out fall leaves, or weed. Pachysandra will spring back from a footstep, ivy never notices, but roses—particularly the Miniatures, which are so often recommended as ground cover—snap and crush.

One rose that will tolerate being stepped on is the Asian species *R. wichuraiana.* This vigorous, sprawling plant forms a hardy and disease-resistant carpet of glossy, almost evergreen foliage and single white flowers. It is planted around a boulder at the NYBG, where it still allows passage of gardeners without significant damage.

If you are determined to use roses as a ground cover, then Ruggiero recommends that you keep the bed small, small enough that you can reach in to weed or clip without actually stepping on the plants. But even then, he believes you will be making a mistake. "To me a ground cover is something you put in; you forget about." And roses—even the hardiest species—are not low-maintenance plants.

Planting in masses, in formal beds, is the traditional way to display roses, and if properly managed such a display can be very effective. It requires a serious commitment, however. Creating a formal rose bed necessitates setting aside a substantial area of open, sunny, and preferably level ground. There is a heavy investment in nursery stock initially, since to have an impact, a rose bed must be densely planted. Finally, bedding demands conscientious and consistent maintenance, for nothing looks worse than a bed of poorly pruned, disease-stricken rosebushes.

But if you are equal to this investment of time and resources, a bed (or beds) of roses offers a kind of visual impact that almost no other garden feature can equal. When in full bloom, a solid phalanx of everblooming modern roses is quite simply glorious. Indeed, it is in this situation that Hybrid Tea roses, Floribundas, Grandifloras, and many of the Miniature roses show to best advantage.

The modern everbloomers are the roses of choice for bedding not only because they rebloom more consistently but also because they respond well to severe pruning. A bed looks far more impressive when all the roses have been trained to the same height and so, visually at least, merge into a solid block.

Rose bed basics. When designing a rose bed, above all let practical considerations be your guide. Since in order to keep the soil light and well aerated it's necessary to avoid stepping into the bed, keep the planting no wider than your reach. This will ensure that even the roses at the bed's center can be pruned or deadheaded when you are standing outside its edge.

Because the average reach of an adult is about 3 feet, Mike Ruggiero uses that as the basic unit in designing a bed. If the planting will be accessible from both sides, he will make a bed as much as 6 feet deep; if it is accessible from only one side (as in the case of a bed planted against the foundation of a house), then he makes the bed no more than 3 feet deep. The length of a bed is limited only by the size of the garden and by personal preference.

Point of view should also be taken into account when you are designing a bed, for it will determine how you arrange different kinds of roses within this planting. Generally, Ruggiero advises setting the lowest-growing roses—Miniatures, for example—at the edge of the bed closest to the viewer and setting behind them the medium-size roses such as Floribundas, arranging the tallest roses such as Hybrid Teas at the back. This sort of arrangement makes it easy to see all the flowers, and it gives a sense of visual movement to the bed. Planting shorter roses toward either end, too, will also give the bed a visual sweep and make it look more rooted into the landscape.

Because your visitors are mobile, point of view will constantly change, but a bed will usually have one perspective from which it is most often viewed. A bed that runs along a path, for instance, will be most often viewed from the path, while a border of roses running around a patio will be most often viewed from the pavement. If you are planting several beds together, you may wish to create a feeling of enclosure by arranging the beds to be viewed from a central point.

ROOM OF THEIR OWN: SPACING

Another design element that you must consider when planning a bed is the amount of space each rosebush will require. If planted too close together, the roses will appear crowded, and the risk of fungal diseases will be increased. If planted too far apart, the bed will look spotty and sparse. So each rose needs to be set at the proper interval from its neighbor; but how far is that?

The object should always be to set the roses just close enough in the bed that they merge into a solid mass but not so close that they become entangled. The correct interval will vary both with the type of rose you choose to grow (obviously a Miniature will need less space than a full-size Hybrid Tea) and with the individual cultivar. For example, 'Swarthmore', a pink-flowered Hybrid Tea, has a distinctly upright habit of growth, and it should be planted at a somewhat closer interval than average; say, 2 to $2\frac{1}{2}$ feet. A more spreading cultivar such as 'Precious Platinum', a red-flowered Hybrid Tea, would require 3 or, better yet, $3\frac{1}{2}$ feet.

Given the variability of roses, a list of numbers is of little help. Mike Ruggiero recommends that after you choose the roses you want to plant in your bed, you make a trip to a public rose garden and observe firsthand the pattern of growth that each rose cultivar follows. Take that information home with you, and then adjust it, if necessary, to suit your needs. If you are growing roses for exhibition, or primarily as a source of cut flowers, you will probably prune even more severely than usual: the finest blossoms are borne on bushes that have been cut back to no more than four canes. Roses maintained in this fashion will have to be set extra close in the bed if they are to fill in the space at all, and like all cutting beds, it may never succeed in becoming equally useful ornamentally.

COMBINING COLORS AND TEXTURES

In any type of garden, some of the most satisfying rewards result from hitting on a winning combination of colors or plant combinations. Often even the experts owe these successes to happy accident, but sometimes such a success is the result of good planning. Ruggiero offers an example: "In the fragrant Floribunda area I didn't want to put a yellow rose next to a pink; so I put a yellow next to a peach, because the peach has yellow in it." The choice seems obvious when put this way, but often combining colors is more difficult. Ruggiero recommends going to the art supply store and buying an inexpensive color wheel, so that you can visually compare different colors and see if a given combination pleases the eye. You too can take your cues from the rose's coloring.

When even the best planning fails and a gardener finds him- or herself with two or more bushes side by side whose flower colors do not harmonize, there is another solution: a continuous edging of some other plant to pull together all the roses within a bed. In the NYBG rose garden, where tests mean planting a huge number of different and often discordant colors in the same bed, Ruggiero has edged all the outer beds of the rose garden with a low hedge of catmint. The silvery green foliage and light blue flowers of this plant seem to harmonize

Golden lemon thyme becomes a striking underplanting for the Gallica rose 'La Belle Sultane'. When planting roses among herbs, use only disease-resistant cultivars; spraying the rose with pesticide will destroy the herbs' culinary value.

with any color of rose, and the continuity it provides prevents the garden from breaking up into visually warring factions.

"Our roses are all different colors, so the catmint is the one thing that fuses them all together. You'll have a purple rose next to a maroon rose next to a yellow; the catmint color pulls it together. It binds it. If you tried to use a lot of different types or colors of edging, it would look mismatched."

Underplanting ideas. The NYBG also uses a variety of underplantings to achieve the same, unifying effect. Pansies are set out under the roses in the fall—they overwinter to provide a colorful floor the next spring and summer. Sweet alyssum and portulaca seeds scattered under the roses also fill in the blanks. Ruggiero prefers white-flowered cultivars of these annuals so that when they spread and bloom, the roses seem to emerge from a froth of white. The portulaca 'White Swan', which bears double white flowers, is particularly attractive, bloom-

A well-planned carpet of variegated sedum acts as a cool foil for the warm pink blossoms of 'Betty Prior'; the sedum's shallow roots do not compete with those of the rose.

ing all summer and then self-sowing to return the following spring.

When installing an underplanting, be careful not to plant something that will compete with the roses. An edging hedge such as catmint can be set out beyond the roses' roots, so that unless it has really aggressive roots, it won't bother the bushes within. But for an underplanting, it is essential to select something shallow-rooted. Otherwise, the underplanting will rob the roses of water and nutrients.

As always, the best advice to home-garden designers is to borrow freely—from gardens of talented neighbors, from gardens visited on their travels, from public gardens, and from books—and then improvise. Another gardener might, for example, be plagued with the problem of keeping disease-prone *R. glauca* beautiful all summer. By the midsummer, when the fungal diseases have robbed the rosebushes of their foliage, interplanted clematises

Twine honeysuckle up through a shrub rose? "Take a chance," advises Mike Ruggiero. Unusual pairings of plants and colors create fun, almost improvisational gardens.

can fill them with another kind of blossom and leaves. Or a purple-leaved honeysuckle, *Lonicera × heckrottii*, woven up through a white-flowered climbing rose in a flamboyant combination makes a stunning garden design.

The most unusual rose planting Mike Ruggiero has ever seen was in a garden in England. There, red-flowered roses were interplanted with a red-leaved form of the bold, subtropical foliage plant *Canna*. The effect was . . . "shocking."

"Take a chance" is his advice. Remember that gardens are not cast in stone; you can always replant. Your first effort may need adjustment, but it may also be a garden innovation that will inspire other gardeners.

Rosa Damascena.   *Rosier de Cels.*

4
GETTING
STARTED

O nce you've decided how to integrate roses with the rest of your plantings, the next step is to select the shrubs. As with any other aspect of rose growing, these tasks demand a certain skill.

There are two primary sources of rosebushes: local nurseries and garden centers, and mail-order nurseries. Both have advantages and disadvantages.

SHOPPING FOR ROSES—LOCAL NURSERIES

If you shop at local nurseries, you will be able to personally select the plants you buy, but the selection of cultivars from which you will be choosing is likely to be very limited. "None of the local nurseries I've been to sell the Kordesii rose 'Illusion'," Mike Ruggiero points out. Although this red rose is not a popular success, he has found it to be exceptionally well adapted to the New York metropolitan area, a very hardy rambler that is a reliable bloomer. "The local nurseries will have the David Austin roses, but because they buy their roses from one wholesaler, they'll have only the David Austin roses that wholesaler carries. Through mail order, though, you can get anything."

So would he ever buy a rose at the garden center down the street? If he wants to shop anytime but early spring or early fall, he has little choice. Mail-order nurseries most often ship their roses "bare-root" (without any soil around the roots). This can only be done when the rose is dormant, and the dormant plants should be set back in the ground early on in the growing season, around the time they would normally awaken, open their buds, and start to grow. To buy roses later in the growing season, you must buy container-grown plants (rose-bushes growing in pots). These can be transplanted into the garden virtually anytime the ground is not frozen, although a midsummer planting is not ideal. You pay extra for this flexibility—container-grown roses are far more expensive than bare-root roses purchased through the mail—but then, convenience generally comes at a cost.

Along with flexibility, shopping for roses at the local garden center allows you to inspect each plant before you buy, and what you find in the course of such an inspection can be very revealing. Besides looking for the obvious signs of health—good leaf color; thick, sturdy canes without signs of bruising or damage—you should check the foliage to make sure it is disease-free, and check under the leaves and along the stems for any insect pests lurking there. Then, if the nurseryman will permit, turn the rose on its side and knock it out of its pot.

As sources for rosebushes, local nurseries, garden centers, and mail-order nurseries have disadvantages as well as advantages. Choosing demands a certain skill.

Loosen and then gently slide the plant's root ball far enough out of the container so that you can see the roots, or at least the area where the roots ought to be. If the plant has been well cared for, it should have roots reaching right out to the edge of the soil—you should be able to see their white tips. Make sure that no areas of the roots are black. This kind of discoloration is typical of plants that have been left out in the hot sun, so that the roots have been cooked. Often the roses in the back of a display have healthier root systems, because their pots have been sheltered from the sun by the pots in front of them.

Because potted roses are usually in full growth by the time the customer buys them, the initial pruning of the bushes has already been done by the nurseryman. The skill with which this has been done is a good indication of the caliber of care the roses have received in general. Ideally, the pruning should have given the potted roses a good structure for future development: they should have an open center surrounded by three to five canes whose growth is directed outward. These canes should be

> *Some nurseries won't remove any cane from a plant because they want a bigger plant and they want to impress you with a lot of canes. With roses, if the center's clogged, it's not a good plant.*

evenly spaced around the plant, they should be thick and substantial, and each should have three to five actively growing buds.

Beware the big, overly lush potted rosebush, Mike Ruggiero advises. "Some nurseries won't remove any cane from a plant because they want a bigger plant and they want to impress you with a lot of canes. With roses, if the center's clogged, it's not a good plant. What happens when you have a plant with 10 to 12 canes is that they all produce weak growth because they all rely on the very limited and traumatized root system for water and nutrients. If, on that same plant, you later go in and remove the center yourself, you'll find that what's left is very spindly. The nursery is not doing you any favors by leaving the center canes."

SHOPPING FOR ROSES—BY MAIL

When ordering roses from mail-order nurseries, there is no opportunity for inspection before the purchase, so buying the best plants means relying on the integrity of the firm. As in every other aspect of modern life, integrity in nurseries is not as sure a thing as it once was. Until a few decades ago the nursery trade was dominated by stable family-owned firms, but today it is an industry of big businesses with all the corporate takeovers, acquisitions, and spinoffs that occur in other such industries. The big rose nurseries are continually changing ownership and management. Though a family name may remain with a business, most often the original owners no longer have any association with the firm, and profit may have replaced quality as the primary goal.

It is not uncommon for some very prestigious nurseries to ship mislabeled plants; Mike Ruggiero recalls one time when he ordered a Rugosa rose and received a Bourbon instead. "Not even close," he chides. A novice might not have recognized the substitution, but surely he or she would have wondered why the new rose didn't perform as advertised. Ruggiero also knows of a well-respected firm that commonly sends out rosebushes infected with mosaic virus. Within a few years of planting, the bushes lose vigor and die. Unfortunately, novices may blame their own lack of horticultural skill for the losses, never realizing that they were doomed to failure by the carelessness of the nurseryman.

There are two ways to avoid these kinds of disappointment. One is talk to more experienced rose gardeners and ask them which companies they recommend. The second is to place a small order with a company first, and then if you are pleased with the quality of the roses they ship you, you can place a larger order later and be relatively assured that you'll be satisfied with what you will get.

OWN-ROOT VERSUS GRAFTED ROSES

Nurserymen usually propagate roses in two ways. The more common method is to take a bud from a desirable cultivar and graft it onto a tough but unattractive "rootstock" rose. This produces a plant that is, in effect, a partnership: the rootstock's roots support the handsomer flowers, foliage, and fruits of the garden rose.

A less common method of propagating roses, one that is used almost exclusively with old garden roses, is to root a cutting from the parent bush. This results in a plant that is all of the same genetic makeup: the roots are of the same type of rose as the top growth. Such bushes are generally called "own-root roses," and they offer some distinct advantages.

From a nurseryman's point of view, grafted roses are desirable because the plants get off to a very fast start. The roots spread rapidly through the soil, encouraging vigorous growth in the rose above the graft, and the whole is ready to be shipped to market well before an own-root rose propagated at the same time. But grafted roses have a disadvantage from the gardener's point of view: if anything should happen to the top growth—if, for instance, an unseasonable frost should kill the rose back to the "bud union" (the point where the hybrid's bud was grafted onto the rootstock)—then the desirable, hybrid plant is essentially dead. New growth may emerge from the bush's roots, but these new shoots will be growth of the rootstock rose and will bear its coarse, inferior foliage and flowers.

It is not uncommon for some very prestigious nurseries to ship mislabeled plants; Mike Ruggiero recalls one time when he ordered a Rugosa rose and received a Bourbon instead.

If a similar misfortune should befall an own-root rose, the growth that emerges from its roots will be of the desirable, garden-type rose. An own-root rose may be slower-growing initially (and typically these plants are smaller and less robust than grafted plants at the time of purchase), but it is also a far more durable plant. Own-root specimens of the modern roses are, however, virtually unobtainable.

"Suckers" on grafted roses. Grafted bushes make fine plants, of course, but at a price. From time to time a shoot may emerge from the rootstock. These so-called reversions, or suckers, are easy to spot because the canes are faster-growing, almost thornless, and usually a different color from the garden rose that was grafted on top of the rootstock. Remove suckers as soon as you find them, for otherwise they may overwhelm the top half of the grafted partnership. The appearance of semidouble, dusky maroon flowers on long arching canes is a sure sign of this, for they belong to 'Dr. Huey', a turn-of-the-century climbing rose that is the most commonly used rootstock today.

Removing a sucker is fairly easy, but it must be done correctly. Dig around the base of the sucker with a trowel until you expose the spot where it sprouts from a root. Then cut the sucker off as close to the root as you can and replace the soil, both to eliminate the existing sucker and to prevent it from resprouting.

Besides 'Dr. Huey', some nurseries also graft onto seedling plants of *R. multiflora* or *R. canina*. Mike Ruggiero actually keeps a specimen of *R. canina* in the NYBG rose garden to use in demystifying supposed cases of reversion. Some rosarians buy only plants grafted onto particular rootstocks, because they believe that roses grafted onto these will perform better in their garden, but Ruggiero believes that roses in good condition flourish or fail because of the care they receive, not because of their rootstock.

PLANTING ROSES

If you did not have your soil tested when you were choosing a site for your rose plantings (see chapter 2), be sure to do it before you plant. In fact, it's advisable to have another test done if a year or more has passed since the last test, as the fertilizers and organic matter applied since the first test may have markedly changed the soil's character or may have washed away or decomposed.

Soil testing. At the Peggy Rockefeller Rose Garden, Mike Ruggiero has the soil from three or four different spots within the garden tested annually. These tests are always "comprehensive" ones and analyze the samples not only for the levels of the three major plant elements (nitrogen, phosphorus, and potassium) but also for organic makeup and micronutrient content. And because he always includes the information that roses will be grown in that soil, the soil-testing laboratory knows to test for magnesium, an element that is present in tiny amounts (usually referred to as a "trace element") but that nevertheless is very important to the health of roses. "Magnesium helps improve the structure of the canes and the vigor and height of the plant. It will make your roses grow bigger, faster, and better." If the soil test indicates a deficiency of magnesium, he scatters Epsom salts over the soil around each plant: he may give each mature Hybrid Tea a half-cup dose of the salts. The response to this treatment is quick. Typically, he says, you can see an improvement in the rose's vigor right away.

The lab report will usually include recommendations for amounts of nutrients to be applied to the soil, and it should also note the soil's pH—its alkalinity or acidity. The ideal pH for roses lies somewhere between 6.5 and 6.8. If the reading for your soil is lower than this, you should add lime to make the soil less acid; if your reading is higher, you may have to apply some formulation of sulfur to make the soil less alkaline.

Preparing the soil. These tests become the blueprint for tailoring fertilization and maintenance programs, ensuring that roses aren't overdosed with one nutrient and underdosed with another. But the soil tests are also a guide to proper soil preparation at planting time, and that is crucial. Once a rose is in the ground and growing, digging around it would injure its roots. So if your soil is deficient in organic matter, before planting is the time to improve it, when any amendments can be mixed all thoughout the soil the rose roots will penetrate. That's why Ruggiero recommends digging rose beds to a depth of 2 feet.

Mix phosphates into the soil before planting the rose—this is a nutrient that doesn't move easily through the soil and won't provide much benefit if sprinkled onto the soil surface afterward.

For roses that are being integrated into an existing landscape as individual shrubs, he advises excavating a planting hole of the same depth and 2 feet wide. The extra work up front pays ample dividends later on as the roses develop into healthier, more self-sufficient bushes.

What exactly you add to the soil at planting time will depend on the quality of your soil, as assessed by the lab tests. As a rule, though, organic material such as dehydrated cow manure blended with a little sphagnum peat is a good idea, as well as a bit of phosphorus, which roses need for healthy root growth. Phosphorus doesn't move easily through the soil, however, and if applied to the soil surface, it doesn't penetrate down to the root zone. So take care to mix superphosphate—and any amendments—all through the soil at planting time. Instead of simply dumping the amendments into the bottom of the planting hole, fork a bit into the hole, but mix most of it thoroughly with the soil excavated from the hole, since that is what is replaced around the rose's roots.

Although the soil-test laboratory may recommend heavy fertilization at planting time, Ruggiero prefers to let the roots establish themselves in their new home first. Aside from the superphosphate, he reserves the recommended fertilizers, instead watering in new bushes at planting time with one of the commercially available "plant starters." These are water soluble and provide a little nitrogen, which promotes leaf and stem growth. By June, the new bushes are ready for the regularly scheduled feedings that he administers to all the roses.

Spring vs. fall planting. In most areas of the country, planting is best done either in the spring or fall. Mike has done both. This has been out of necessity. When he is ordering something rare from a specialty grower, Ruggiero has found that it pays to order (and plant) in fall, because fewer gardeners order roses then. With less competition, he is more likely to get what he wants; if he waits until spring, the growers may have sold out the more popular items. Nevertheless, he advises that spring planting generally offers a better rate of success in cold-climate areas, since the new bushes will have longer to settle in before winter attacks them. In regions with hot summers and mild winters, however, fall planting is advantageous, since it gives the bushes longer to repair damage to their roots before the onslaught of hot weather.

If he is planting bare-root roses that he has ordered through the mail, Ruggiero prepares the soil before the dormant bushes arrive, so that there will be no unnecessary delays in getting them into the ground. But he doesn't take the bushes out of the shipping carton and plant right away.

A bath for bare-root roses. First, the roses get a bath. A common recommendation is to soak bare-root roses in water for 2 to 4 hours before planting; he soaks his roses for 24 hours in a tub of water outdoors, and to give the new bushes a little boost, he adds fish emulsion to the water at a rate of 1 teaspoon per 20 gallons. He dunks each bush as he puts it in the tub to wash it free of soil—bare-root roses are sometimes buried in soil at the nursery for storage and commonly arrive thoroughly muddy. Cleaning the roses may not be essential, but he believes it can't hurt and it's easy enough to do as part of the soaking process.

After the bath, the roses are pruned of any dead canes, and if the rosebush wasn't pruned at the nursery (most bushes are pruned before shipping), Ruggiero cuts it back to three to five canes and three to five buds per cane, just as with potted roses. Bare-root roses can arrive with roots 3 feet long; he cuts such overlong roots back by half and at the

Ruggiero has found that it pays to order (and plant) in fall, because fewer gardeners order roses then. With less competition, he is more likely to get what he wants.

same time prunes away any broken or obviously dead roots. Trimming the roots in this fashion is partly a matter of removing damaged and unhealthy tissue, but it also stimulates the bush to form a denser network of fibrous "feeder roots" all around the plant.

The planting. Finally, the rose is ready to plant. The planting procedure is somewhat different for bare-root roses than for container-grown ones, and in fact this is another area where the bare-root plants offer an advantage. Because the bare-root rose's roots are free of soil and exposed, you can make sure that they end up spread evenly around the planting hole. With container-grown roses, you have to trust the nurseryman who potted them.

To plant a bare-root rose, build a cone of soil in the bottom of the planting hole, and set the rose on top of it, spreading its roots out around the cone and downward like a skirt. Position the rose so that the bud union (the swollen knot of wood where the canes join the rootstock) sits about an inch below ground level. This gives the bud union a bit of protection from winter cold and helps ensure that the rose won't be winterkilled back to the rootstock. Ruggiero hastens to add,

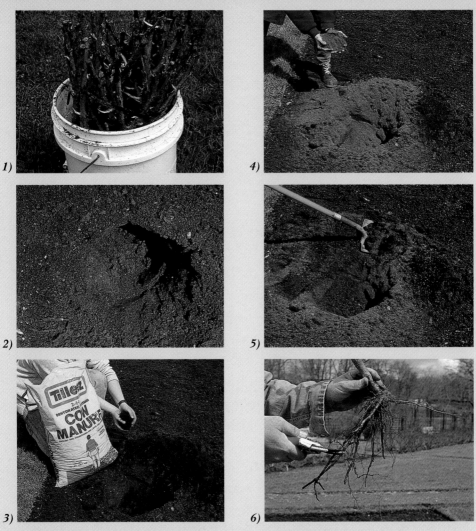

1) **Soak the roots** of the bushes in water for 4–6 hours before planting.

2) **Choose a site** that has well-drained soil and begin the soil preparation by digging a hole 18 inches wide and deep.

3) **Add soil amendments** such as well-rotted cow manure, compost, peat moss, etc., to the soil in the hole and the soil that was removed from the hole.

4) **Add to the soil** superphosphate (0-46-0) or bone meal (1-11-0) to aid the plant in establishing a good root system. Complete fertilizers that contain nitrogen can be used after the plant has produced roots and foliage.

5) **Turn the soil** until the amendments become thoroughly incorporated.

6) **Remove any broken or damaged parts** of the root system and reduce the roots by a third.

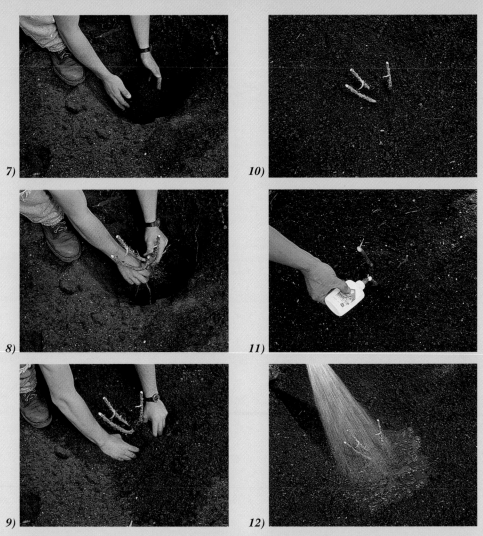

7) **Mound the soil** in the center of the hole into a small pyramid.

8) **Place the base** of the rosebush on the pyramid and spread its roots out away from the center.

9) **Backfill the hole** while holding the rose in place and firmly pack the soil around the roots.

10) **Cover the graft union** with soil to prevent dehydration. If your soil is deep and well-drained you can plant the bush with the graft union just below the surface of the soil.

11) **Use nontoxic wood glue** to seal the cuts made on the canes.

12) **Water thoroughly.**

1) *Make sure the structure is good and the foliage is clean and healthy when you are purchasing a potted rose.*

2) *Choose a site that has well-drained soil and begin the soil preparation by digging a hole 18 inches wide and deep.*

3) *Add soil amendments such as well-rotted cow manure, compost, peat moss, etc., to both the soil in the hole and the soil that was removed. Then turn the soil until the amendments have become thoroughly incorporated.*

4) *Carefully remove the rose from its container. If the roots at the bottom of the soil is compacted into a solid mat, loosen them slightly with your fingers. If it has not, plant the rose with as little disturbance as possible.*

though, that he plants this way only if the soil is well drained. If the soil tends to stay wet, he advises setting the bud union at the same level as the soil surface. Even then, he recommends that the gardener heap some extra soil around the bud union for the first few weeks the rose is in the ground to protect it from dehydration and sunburn.

After positioning the rose, it's time to refill the hole with amended soil. Firm that in around the roots with your fingers—don't

5) Place the rose into the hole so that the soil level of the root ball is at or just below the level of the hole.

6) Backfill the soil while holding the rose at the proper level.

7) Firmly pack the soil.

8) Level the soil and then water well.

use your heel to pack in the soil, since that will compress it too tightly. Water well, and the job is done.

If you are planting a container-grown rose, you simply tip the pot on its side and slip the root ball out. If the root ball is at all difficult to extract, don't force it; instead, use a pair of tin snips or a pair of shears to cut off the container.

Once the root ball is out, set it into the prepared planting hole, again taking care to position it in the hole so that the bud union rests about an inch below the soil in a well-drained site, at soil level in less than ideally drained soil. Refill the hole with amended soil, firming it in around the root ball with your fingertips, and water well.

Special situations. Sometimes rosebushes are offered for sale with their roots packed in cardboard boxes filled with peaty soil. Ruggiero dislikes this type of packaging, because instructions printed on the side usually advise planting the new bush box and all, a practice that discourages quick rooting and adaptation. It has been Mike's experience that being encased in the box discourages the rose from rooting into its new home, so he advises gardeners to do one of two things. If the boxed rose is to be planted early in the spring, while the plant is still dormant, he suggests simply removing it from the box and treating it like a regular bare-root rose. If the boxed rose has broken dormancy

Though the product label advises planting roses such as these with boxes intact, Mike Ruggiero believes that this deters the bushes from rooting into the soil properly.

and is actively growing, cut off the bottom of the box and set the rose in the planting hole. Then cut a slit through the side of the box and remove the cardboard from around the root ball, taking care to disturb the roots as little as possible. Refill the hole as usual.

AFTERCARE

The special care required by new roses doesn't end as soon as they are in the ground. For example, the new bushes will require extra irrigation; Mike Ruggiero suggests watering them two to three times as often as you water established roses. Established bushes, after all, have spread a network of roots out around their bases to harvest any moisture that might be in that broad expanse of soil. Newly planted roses haven't yet developed this extensive root system and so are much more liable to dehydrate. Mulching—often suggested as a means of reducing plants' need for irrigation—will help drought-proof established rosebushes. But while a blanket of mulch will keep the soil cooler and moister, it can't substitute for the roots a newly planted rose doesn't have. And neglecting the watering in the first few months after planting a rose will have effects that may last for years. In Ruggiero's experience, which he can back up with the results of scientific studies, a plant whose growth is checked in its early life may not die, but it never recovers full vigor.

"Pay attention" is the best advice. Recent transplants are especially sensitive to stresses in their environment. So check them regularly and look for the visual signals that communicate their needs. This is a basic horticultural skill, and perhaps the most important.

"I've noticed that the people who have good luck with plants often are the immigrants from agricultural countries," Mike Ruggiero observe. "They don't know the name of anything, but they're giving the plant what it needs, because they're looking at the plant. They know through observation how to grow it. If the plant looks wilted, they give it water. It's not luck—it's good care."

Forget "green thumbs." Success doesn't come from green thumbs; it comes from giving a plant the best start you can—and paying attention.

Rosa Indica.

Rosier des Indes jaune.

P. J. Redouté

Bessin

5
PRUNING AND WINTER PROTECTION

etting the plants off to a good start is an essential first step to beautiful, healthy roses, but it is only the first step. Equally important is what comes after: the kind of care they receive once they are in the ground. Roses (when well grown) are among the most rewarding of garden shrubs, but they also require more attention than most other kinds of garden shrubs. The work involved must be done right, and it must be done in a timely fashion. If your roses are to look their best, the care must be consistent.

For the most part, rose care is similar to that of other garden shrubs. Water roses regularly during dry spells throughout the growing season, giving each shrub as much as an inch of water a week during the hot weeks of midsummer. Keep the beds free of weeds—an organic mulch spread over their roots is helpful here. Deadhead frequently unless you plan to harvest hips. All of these are procedures familiar to any experienced gardener, even one who has never grown roses before.

Besides this generic kind of maintenance, however, roses also have some special requirements, and to keep them in the full flush of health calls for some special skills that can make rose growing seem intimidating for the average gardener. In truth, these special skills are easily learned.

PRUNING

An unpruned rosebush soon becomes an unhealthy and flowerless rosebush, but rose pruning is also the primary subject of confusion among novice rose gardeners. Gardeners who feel confident pruning virtually every other kind of shrub or tree often hesitate to undertake the training of their roses.

The art of pruning, according to Mike Ruggiero, lies in paying attention to how the plant wants to grow and enhancing that with shears and saw. There is no one right way to prune roses: different types of roses grow very differently and so must be pruned differently. Even the briefest of walks around the Peggy Rockefeller Rose Garden reveals that roses are a diverse group—and it's fairly obvious that a huge old Shrub rose, with its arching, spreading canes, requires a different kind of pruning than a Hybrid Tea, with its upright, angular ones. Ruggiero agrees that a gardener could prune these two roses in the same way—but doing so would destroy the health and appearance of one or both the shrubs.

Of course, many of the fundamental goals remain the same no matter what kind of rose you are pruning. As with any shrub, when pruning roses you want to promote not only abundant flowering but also a sturdy, well-spaced framework of branches that permits air to circulate through the center of the plant—that helps keep the plant pest- and disease-free. How you accomplish these goals, though, will vary with the kind of rose.

Observing the gardeners pruning at a public rose garden is one of the best ways to learn pruning techniques, but even if you can't time your visit with pruning day, a public garden is still a good teacher. Find specimens of the roses you are growing. If you can't locate exact matches, at least try to locate roses of the same class. Note how the gardeners have pruned these plants. If you visit the garden late in the season, after the roses have made their new growth, the results of the pruning may not be so apparent. But even then, you can gather useful information about how the plants want to grow. If, for example, you find a match for one of your roses, and the plant in the public garden has grown into a tall, long-caned shrub, almost a climber, then you know that you should not try to maintain yours as a compact bedding plant. Similarly, there is no point trying to train a compact Hybrid Rugosa to ramble along a rail fence. You can't change a rose's natural form; to try to do so will only destroy the plant's beauty.

TOOLS

To prune well, you need the right tools. Mike Ruggiero recommends three items as essential: a pair of hand pruning shears, a pair of lopping shears, and a narrow-tipped handsaw. All three tools should be of excellent quality.

Pruning shears should be the bypass type, with blades that cut like scissors. The less expensive anvil-type shears, which have a sharp blade that cuts by squeezing the branch against a flat "anvil," are adequate for many other kinds of pruning, but not for roses, according to Ruggiero. That's because most rose pruning is done in spring, when the rosebush's cambium (the green and growing tissue right under the bark) is loose and slips easily from the cane.

Roses, when they are well grown, are among the most rewarding of garden shrubs, but they also require more attention.

The squeezing action of the anvil pruners "mashes" this cambium, and the cut cane eventually dies back at the tip as a result. In contrast, the blades of bypass pruners, if they are sharp, slip right through.

Of the many kinds of lopping shears on the market, Ruggiero favors the lightweight aluminum models. He has noticed that these promote cleaner cuts, because they are easier to wield. A gardener trying to manipulate the heavier loppers with steel or wooden handles might lose his balance and fall into the rose's thorny embrace; so the tendency is to lean back and prune from long distance, reaching in with the lopper blades to grab and twist—ripping off branches rather than cutting clean. With the lightweight aluminum loppers, the gardener is able to lean into the work; he can get into the heart of the bush and snip cleanly and precisely at the right spot.

Finally, Ruggiero recommends buying a pruning saw with a curved, tapered blade. The narrow tip of this tool can be slipped in among the canes right at the base of a bush and so is ideal for removing older canes neatly and completely. A squarer saw blade cannot be insinuated among the canes as successfully and so tends to leave stumps; stumps sprout suckers to crowd the bush with weak and undesirable growth.

It is extremely important to make sure that your tools are sharp. Buy hand pruners with replaceable blades if you can, so that each year you start the pruning season with a brand-new, relatively inexpensive blade. Keep old blades, though, for cutting away the thick, woody, dead canes; dry wood is harder and can chip a blade.

Ruggiero seldom wears gloves when he is pruning roses; he likes to be able to feel as well as see what he is doing. But he keeps a pair on hand, and he makes sure that they are thick leather gloves with gauntlets that protect his wrists and lower arms. He puts these on when he must prune some of the really vigorous, well-armed roses such as the old climbing rose 'Silver Moon',

Observing the gardeners pruning at a public rose garden is one of the best ways to learn pruning techniques.

which has thick canes and huge thorns. Don't bother with cloth gloves, he adds—you might as well wear nothing at all.

One final "tool" in Ruggiero's pruning kit is a tube of carpenter's white glue. After every cut he makes, he seals the wound with a squeeze of glue. The glue is cheap, convenient, and nontoxic, and this method is very effective at excluding stem borers. Borers are the larvae of a variety of flying insects, which can gain access to the rose stems through the pruning wounds and burrow down into the canes below, causing the plants to die back. The glue, which dries clear, makes an effective barrier.

TAKING THE CONFUSION OUT OF PRUNING

Part of the reason that rose pruning is so confusing to the average gardener is a matter of semantics. We include many different kinds of plants under the title "roses": climbers, bedding shrubs, hedge shrubs, once-blooming plants, and everbloomers. Each has its own pattern of growth, but to most home gardeners, a rose is a rose, and it seems logical to treat them all alike. Yet learning to distinguish rose from rose is the basis of successful pruning.

It is not absolutely essential to know what cultivar you have, but you should know its class, or at the very least, its general type—whether it is an old-fashioned, once-blooming rose, or a modern, everblooming variety. Pruning will also be influenced by the time of year: different types of pruning are appropriate for different seasons.

Pruning modern everblooming roses. Hybrid Teas, Floribundas, Grandifloras, and Miniatures produce the finest flowers on new wood—that is, on branches and canes formed since the bushes emerged from dormancy that spring. To ensure a good crop of flowers, these classes of roses are cut back relatively severely every year in early spring, at the beginning of the growing season. This forces the bushes to make lots of new growth, setting the stage for a first-class floral display.

Although this major pruning is always done in spring, its exact schedule is dictated not by the calendar but by the rosebushes themselves. Some rosarians advocate a very early pruning; they make their cuts as the buds begin to swell. (It is essential to wait at least that long, because only when the rose begins new growth can you tell which canes have been killed by winter weather and have to be removed entirely.) Mike Ruggiero likes to wait a little longer. Cutting back the old canes actually stimulates the new growth and brings the rosebushes out of dormancy faster. That can set the bush up for disaster if there is a late cold snap, since the newly emerging growth is particularly prone to frost damage. Given the vagaries of a northeastern spring, he likes to let the roses emerge from dormancy at their own rate. He doesn't prune until the new leaves and stems are $\frac{1}{2}$ to 1 inch long. By then, the danger of frost is usually past.

1)

2)

3)

4)

1–2) **In spring,** *when buds have begun to expand, carefully remove the winter protection without damaging the canes.*

3) **Wash the remaining** *winter protection off of the canes to expose the buds.*
4) **Begin pruning** *by removing any dead or damaged wood.*

The pruning that should be done at planting time was detailed in the last chapter; the pruning required by an established bush, one that has been in the ground a year or more, is fairly similar. Begin by removing all dead or injured canes, cutting these off at their bases with hand pruners, loppers, or a saw, depending on their size. Next remove any spindly or weak canes that are crowding the center of the bush: the object is to leave three to five canes that are evenly spaced around the

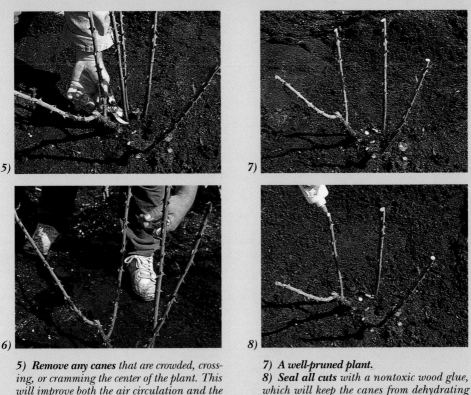

5) Remove any canes that are crowded, crossing, or cramming the center of the plant. This will improve both the air circulation and the amount of light the new growth receives while also helping to control fungus diseases.

6) Shorten the canes to 3 to 7 buds per cane. Leaving 3 or fewer buds will usually produce fewer but larger exhibition-quality flowers, while 5 to 7 buds usually produces more flowers on a bushier plant.

7) A well-pruned plant.

8) Seal all cuts with a nontoxic wood glue, which will keep the canes from dehydrating and help stop stem borers from entering the canes.

bush and all growing more or less outward from the center. Cut these remaining canes back so that each has just three to five outward-facing, actively growing buds.

This sounds like a drastic pruning, but in fact leaving five canes with five buds each makes for a plant with 25 canes by midsummer. That's a lot of new growth for any one bush, and this style of pruning works very well for roses planted as a hedge, since it tends to produce thick, lush bushes. In its most relaxed form, it can even produce bushes that are too thick: for a cultivar such as 'Swarthmore' that naturally produces a narrow, upright bush, a 25-cane plant may be too dense a bundle of branches. Roses of this and similar sorts should be cut back to the three-cane minimum.

Just as an upright rose demands some adjustment in the pruning, so does an unusually vigorous rose. 'Folklore' is an orange-flowered Hybrid Tea that, according to Ruggiero, seems to sprout about 80 canes every spring. Such a plant needs extra attention and some return visits with the shears to prevent it from becoming choked with new growth.

Pruning for exhibition. Although ideally pruning should be calcu-

1) A poorly made cut. Although the cut was made away from the bud, funneling water away from the bud seat, the angle of the cut is much too severe and actually precedes the base of the bud. This opens up the wood adjacent to the bud to dehydration and death of the bud will occur.

2) A properly placed cut. This cut is above and away from the bud, yet it does not proceed past the base of the bud.

lated to enhance the natural growth, it can also be used to modify it. That is the role that pruning plays in raising Hybrid Tea, Floribunda, and Grandiflora roses for exhibition at rose shows. The object of this style of cultivation is to produce a small number of large and perfect blooms by channeling all of a bush's energy into a few buds.

Whereas the usual practice when pruning everblooming roses is to leave three to five buds per cane, the rose exhibitor cuts back harder, so that each remaining cane carries just one or two. And the exhibitor leaves fewer canes per plant—no more than three on the average bush. Fewer canes, Mike Ruggiero explains, means thicker, more vigorous ones.

Nor does the pruning stop there. As its new growth reaches upward, a rose naturally begins to sprout side shoots from the main canes; an ordinary gardener would leave most of these side shoots, but the exhibitor removes them, allowing no more than one or two buds per cane. As Ruggiero observes, "You need a lot of plants to get a few roses." Growing roses for show is "a whole different ball game. That's show-and-tell. " But for those whom only perfection will satisfy, a skillfully grown show rose, with its long, straight stem and exquisitely modeled, flawless buds, satisfies like nothing else.

Pruning Modern Shrub roses. Shrub roses bear flowers most heavily on mature stems that have not yet grown too woody and old; to prune them as you would a Hybrid Tea would severely reduce the number of blossoms. Besides, these roses are grown largely for the form of the plant—the compact mass of foliage that they contribute to a border or bed. To prune them back to stubs each spring would destroy that.

So Mike Ruggiero prunes Modern Shrub roses much as he would any other kind of flowering shrub that produces new growth—new stems—mainly from the base. He uses a method that he calls the "one-third" method: each spring, after the new leaves have emerged and expanded, he removes from each Modern Shrub one-third of the oldest canes. To replace them, he chooses an equal number of well-placed, vigorous young canes from those that sprouted the previous year—then removes the rest of the young sprouts. In addition, of course, he removes any dead or damaged branches and any canes that are growing back into the center of the shrub; like an ingrown toenail, the latter would only cause trouble.

The result of this "one-third" treatment is that his Modern Shrub roses are continually renewing themselves. But at the same time, each shrub always retains enough of the substantial mature growth to keep its characteristic, bushy form and to ensure a good crop of flowers.

Pruning old garden roses. Since most of these living antiques grow as well-rounded, attractive shrubs, Mike Ruggiero prunes them in much the same way as he prunes Modern Shrub roses, with a few important differences.

As noted in chapter 1, the old garden roses are not ever-bloomers. Many produce only one flush of flowers each season, typically in late spring or early summer; the others, although they repeat-bloom, also bear the bulk of their flowers in late spring or early summer. The old garden roses also differ from modern everblooming roses in that the branches that flower most heavily are those which the bush produced during the previous year; the current season's growth typically produces no flowers at all. Therefore, to prune an old garden rose back hard in early spring is to ensure that it will bear no flowers that year. Indeed, to prune off *any* healthy branches in early spring is guaranteed to reduce the number of flowers the bush will produce.

So Ruggiero limits his spring pruning of the old garden roses to the removal of winterkilled branches. He waits until after the bushes have borne their heavy, early-summer flush of flowers before making any more cuts. After that first flush, he gives the old garden roses the same "one-third" treatment he gives the Modern Shrub roses. Because many of the old garden roses make very large shrubs and tend to sprawl, he may also cut back the longest of the canes by a third or more to encourage more compact growth. And, of course, he removes weak and spindly canes and those which are growing back through the centers of the shrubs.

This is his standard treatment for old garden roses, but he often adjusts it if the circumstances warrant. If he is training one of the sprawling shrubs as a climber, he allows it fewer canes. By forcing the shrub to put its strength into a smaller number of canes, he encourages it to make each one longer. This is true also of the Modern Shrub roses he sometimes uses as climbers. When he is espaliering it on a fence, he prunes it differently than he does when he is growing it out in the middle of the garden as a shrub.

Pruning climbing roses. Because climbers commonly originate as "sports"—spontaneous mutations of individual branches on established nonclimbing rosebushes—they may belong to almost any class. All climbers are similar, however, in producing the exceptionally long, upright canes that are their defining characteristic. Preserving and enhancing these requires some special pruning.

Climbers of old garden rose types (those that bloom just once a season) Ruggiero prunes hardly at all in the early spring; at that time he removes only winterkilled branches. Even with roses of modern everblooming classes, such as the Hybrid Teas (climbers of this class are sometimes called "large-flowered climbers") and the Floribundas, Ruggiero does not cut the main vertical canes in spring. In early spring he limits his pruning of everblooming climbers to cutting back the side branches; this stimulates the new growth that produces the best flowering on everbloomers.

Just as an upright rose demands some adjustment in the pruning, so does an unusually vigorous-growing rose.

The main pruning of climbing roses comes after the first flush of flowers—the biggest flush in the case of everbloomers and the only one in the case of many old garden rose climbers. This timing is calculated to cause the least interruption on bloom, while still allowing any new growth stimulated by the pruning enough time to harden off before winter.

In this main pruning, which comes in late June or early July, Ruggiero removes any upright canes that are getting old and woody and are producing fewer flowers. To replace the old canes removed in this fashion, he ties in the most vigorous of the new ones sprouting from the roses' bases. Then all unwanted new canes are removed, too.

SUMMER PRUNING FOR CLIMBING ROSES

When the main framework of a climber gets old and very woody, and is growing less and less vigorously, Ruggiero will rejuvenate the rose by bringing in a new cane as a replacement for one of the old ones. Generally, he waits until after the first flush of flowers has passed, however, to do this. Even with everblooming climbers, this first flush of flowers is the plant's greatest single display of the season, and to cut out a major cane in early spring would sadly affect the show.

So he waits until late June or early July to renovate. The new canes are still flexible at that time and can be gently pulled into the desired position. But it is also early enough in the growing season that any new growth forced out by such a major cut will have time to mature and "harden" before the onset of winter.

Deadheading. Deadheading (the removal of fading flowers before the bush can set seed) is really just another form of pruning. It is an essential form, too, if the gardener wants to get the best performance from everblooming and reblooming roses, for once a bush starts making seeds it generally stops making flowers.

A standard recommendation for deadheading is to cut back the flower and the stem below it to an outward-facing bud and a leaf with five leaflets (roses commonly bear leaves of anywhere from three to seven leaflets, and the buds form on the canes at the bases of the leaf stems). According to this rule, the cane should be at least pencil thick at the cut to encourage compact growth.

Mike Ruggiero agrees with this rule, as long as the rosebush is a vigorous plant. If it is a weak one or is recovering from some setback such as an unusually severe winter, to stubbornly adhere to the five-leaflet rule may cause you to cut all the canes back to stubs. Doing that in midseason will rob the plant of the ability to heal itself.

Although we talk of feeding our plants, plants of course feed themselves. Through fertilization, we may provide minerals and building blocks, but the plant assembles these elements into nutrients, in its green tissues, in the leaves and stems. If you deprive a weak plant of its processing centers, it cannot make the food it needs. With a strong plant, you can afford to deadhead more rigorously, and to do so will indeed encourage more compact growth.

How you deadhead may seem like a minor detail, but the cumulative effect is impressive. You remove just a little bit of wood each time, but if the rose is everblooming and flowers all summer long and into the fall, you risk removing more mass of wood, in total, through deadheading than you cut from the bush in the course of the spring pruning.

Own-root roses. Grafted roses have to be treated with a bit of care. Prune them back too hard, and you may remove all the garden cultivar and end up with nothing but rootstock. However, own-root roses—those growing on their own roots—often respond positively to drastic pruning. In fact, Ruggiero recommends this as a way to rejuvenate shrub roses that have grown old and "leggy," with long canes that are growing only at the tip.

Cutting the shrub back almost to the ground in early spring will force out a multitude of new and vigorous shoots. This trick, he has found, works especially well with Rugosa roses.

Fall pruning. Fall is not a season that most rosarians associate with pruning. The conventional wisdom is that once the rose has gone dormant, you might as well wait until spring and see what survives the winter. But Mike Ruggiero holds that a few timely cuts in the fall will help some roses overwinter with far less damage.

In fall he prunes after the first real cold snap, when the rosebushes have shed their leaves and gone totally dormant. To prune any earlier, he explains, might stimulate a late burst of growth that would not harden off before the cold weather settles in. But once the roses are really dormant, then he shortens the canes of the taller modern roses—Hybrid Teas, Floribundas, and Grandifloras—to 3 feet. Some of these roses will send out canes 6 feet long in a single season of growth, and if these are left uncut, a wet snow or an ice storm may pack on so much extra weight that the longer canes snap.

He has seen the canes of the Hybrid Tea 'Folklore' tear off at the graft, causing the death of the plant.

Winterizing roses. Many kinds of roses are relatively invulnerable to cold weather. The species Rugosa roses, for example, are cold-hardy to −40°F, and the Gallica roses are almost as sturdy. Because the repeat-blooming and everblooming roses resulted from crosses with frost-sensitive Asian species, however, most modern classes of roses are considerably less cold-resistant. Hybrid Tea roses, for instance, commonly experience winter cold damage at the New York Botanical Garden, which lies in the relatively temperate region that the U.S. Department of Agriculture has identified as zone 7. If Mike Ruggiero wants to be sure that his Hybrid Teas, Floribundas, and Grandifloras will carry on from year to year, he has to take steps to protect them from the worst of the cold weather.

The best insurance against cold damage is to make sure that the roses go fully dormant at winter's onset. To do this, the first step is to carefully time the end of the fertilizing regimen. At the NYBG, Ruggiero stops regular feeding—a monthly application of a commercial granular fertilizer specially formulated for roses—at the end of July. This is because he wants the growth of his rosebushes to taper off after that date, so that all the new canes will have time to mature and harden off by late fall. (He does, however, spray the bushes with a very mild solution of soluble fertilizer and water—a pint of 20-20-20 fertilizer dissolved in 100 gallons of water—at the end of September, but this is absorbed right through the rose's leaves and provides a short-lived pick-me-up.) And to further encourage dormancy, he stops deadheading the rosebushes after September 1. Letting the plants go to seed helps put an end to new growth and helps harden off existing canes.

Beyond helping roses go dormant, it is also important to provide a bit of protection from the elements. There are a number of popular devices for protecting dormant roses from winter winds and cold. Cones of Styrofoam made especially for this purpose are available from rose nurseries and from many local garden centers. But in Ruggiero's experience, these can hurt as much as they help, for on a sunny winter day, the cones may act like solar collectors, warming the roses inside to well above the freezing point. Then the bushes must undergo the trauma of freezing all over again when the sun sets.

Some gardeners build frames around their rosebushes and fill them with a loose packing of oak leaves, but this method is very time-consuming. Piling a mixture of one-half sandy loam and one-half compost around the base of each bush to a depth of 10 inches provides just as effective protection. A 5-gallon bucketful is usually sufficient for a new (and small) bush, whereas a large, established plant may require 10 gallons. The object is to create a mound about 10 inches tall.

Some gardeners will "hill up" in this fashion with pure compost

Winter has killed back much of the rose's top growth, but when the soil hilled around the base is removed in spring, the base of the canes is found to be green and intact.

or even aged manure, but those materials may hold too much water and can end up encasing the bushes in ice. Other gardeners hill up with pure topsoil, which is effective, but Ruggiero prefers including compost in his mix because it saves him time. Over the course of the winter, some of the nutrients from the compost leach down into the soil to feed the bushes' roots. And there is an additional benefit in springtime, when he pulls the hills away from around the rosebushes. He removes from the garden about half of the hilling material, using it to make potting soil. But he spreads the rest over the rose beds to serve as a mulch. Spread around in this fashion, the compost in the hilling mix adds a bit of humus to the rose beds and saves him the trouble of bringing in organic amendments.

Whatever is used for hilling up has to drain well—a combination of wet and cold is far more damaging to dormant roses than dry cold. Topsoil, or a mix of topsoil and compost, offers not only good drainage but also absorbs and reradiates heat particularly well. During a thaw the hilling mix absorbs the ambient heat, keeping it from reaching the dormant canes inside the hill, and when the temperature plunges back down, the hill releases the heat it has absorbed, slowing the temperature drop inside the hill. The overall effect is to moderate climatic temperature swings, and a steady—even if cold—temperature is the least likely to cause winterkill.

Giving your roses some shelter through the cold months can be a crucial factor in determining whether they will survive.

Aside from a fall pruning, hilling up is all the protection that most roses need. Only one type of rose requires more nurturing: the rose standard. Hilling a rose standard would protect the bottom part of the rootstock trunk, but it would do nothing to shield the cultivated rose that has been grafted to the top of the trunk. So Ruggiero digs up his standards, pots them up in tubs, and moves them into a cold but frost-free root cellar. Homeowners can provide a similar sort of protection by potting the standards after they are leafless and fully dormant and moving them into an unheated but frost-free garage, where the temperatures hover in the high 30s or low 40s. Alternatively, you can dig up the standards after they have gone dormant, lay them down on their sides, and then cover the whole plant with 12 inches of the regular hilling mix.

One final note on winter protection: Where winters are hard yet a modern-rose look and everblooming habit are desired, try the Miniature roses. The hill of earth that protects only the base of a full-size bush may completely cover a Miniature. If necessary, you can easily dig up the Miniatures and overwinter them in pots in some sheltered place.

Giving your roses some shelter through the cold months can be a crucial factor in determining whether or not they will survive until spring. But once again, the decisions made when planning the garden are what really govern success or failure. The roses that suffer tremendous winter damage in a poorly drained garden can flourish next door in a well-drained one. Likewise, the choice of rose cultivars will have a decisive impact on how much winter damage plantings suffer.

Rugosa roses and Hybrid Rugosas never suffer winter damage in the Peggy Rockefeller Rose Garden, even though they are given no protection. 'Carefree Wonder', the pink-flowered modern landscape rose, and 'Escapade', a pink-flowered Floribunda, overwinter reliably without protection, too. In general, the Floribundas are cold-hardier than the Hybrid Teas. 'Honor', a white-flowered Hybrid Tea, commonly dies back to the part of the canes protected by the hilled-up soil. In a garden more exposed to winter winds than the one at the NYBG, or in a more northern garden, 'Honor' would clearly be a bad choice. A far better choice would be the crimson-flowered classic 'Chrysler Imperial' or the white-flowered 'Pascali'.

Gardeners may develop a passion for the beauty of a particular rose, but, Mike Ruggiero notes, you have to be realistic. He knows. 'Sheer Bliss', with its fragrant, palest pink flowers, is a rose he loves. But even with protection, he could never prolong this Hybrid Tea's life beyond two years at NYBG. He doesn't grow it anymore. There are too many fine roses that like the garden just the way it is.

Rosa Kamtschatica.   *Rosier du Kamtschatka.*

6
PESTS AND DISEASES

rom apples to strawberries, all members of the rose family, Rosaceae, share a vulnerability to diseases. "It's a family trait," Mike Ruggiero says. Like all plants, they attract their quota of pests, too. That doesn't mean you can't have healthy roses in your garden. But if you can't bear the presence of pests and diseases, and if you aren't willing to take measures to control them, then "you shouldn't be growing roses."

Having said that, Ruggiero is quick to add that pest and disease control is a fairly minor part of rose growing. At least it is if you manage your plantings skillfully. Although not an advocate of the old-style chemical blitz, he does spray his roses, and he believes it is virtually impossible to grow most roses without spraying—but he does so only at need, and only after doing his "homework."

Homework begins with identifying exactly what sort of pest is causing the damage, in order to choose a spray precisely targeted to control the pest with a minimum impact on other wildlife and the environment in general. The broad-spectrum sprays, which combine many different chemicals for almost any disease or insect that can infest a rose, are too "ham-handed," Mike insists, and are likely to cause as much harm as good. Broad-spectrum sprays commonly not only kill the pest but also slaughter all the beneficial insects on the rosebushes. Beneficial insects, such as lady beetles, feed on other insects, such as aphids, that cause harm to the rosebush. Killing off the beneficial insects causes populations of harmful insects to explode. At NYBG a gardener once sprayed roses with the insecticide acephate and almost immediately produced a tremendous infestation of sap-sucking spider mites. The reason? The insecticide had killed off the predator mites that feed on spider mites. Quite simply, unfocused, broad-spectrum sprays commonly cause more infestations than they cure. The spray can be reapplied to control the new infestations as they arise, but that merely perpetuates the cycle. In the end, the use of broad-spectrum sprays creates a sort of chemical dependency in roses. This is bad for the environment, and makes extra work for the gardener, too.

There is another kind of homework, at least for a responsible gardener. Ruggiero believes that you must look not only for a targeted spray but also for the spray that is the least toxic alternative. "We don't spray any cholinesterase inhibitors" (insecticides such as Diazinon, which attack the nervous system), he explains, "because once inhaled or absorbed through the skin those chemicals stay in the bloodstream a long time." Likewise, the NYBG crew never sprays chemicals that leave residues in the ground. Ruggiero recalls spraying DDT in his younger days: "That stays in the ground 30 to 40 years." Instead, "If you have to spray, use a chemical that is broken down by sunlight or air," such as the botanical insecticide pyrethrum, which starts to decompose into nontoxic elements almost as soon as it is applied. Such a spray won't poison the groundwater, and it is far less likely to harm other insects, birds, or mammals (although pyrethrum will injure fish if applied directly to the water).

Finally, doing your homework means looking for alternatives to

If the first time you see an aphid, you call for a napalm strike, there's something wrong.

spraying. Often an insect infestation or an outbreak of a rose disease can be controlled or at least mitigated by adjusting overall care.

INSECTS

Gardeners, especially beginners, tend to view insects as their greatest enemy. In fact, this is not the case, at least with roses. The sight of a single insect on a rosebush provokes a defensive reflex in many gardeners, but it's usually an overreaction. "If the first time you see an aphid, you call for a napalm strike, there's something wrong." If the population of insects threatens to affect a plant's form, function, and life—for example, if the insects are causing major defoliation or killing the canes, are preventing the bush from producing flowers and foliage, are in danger of killing the rosebush altogether—then spray. But if you catch an infestation when it is still small, you can probably control it satisfactorily by handpicking. If you find six aphids on a plant, simply squash them between thumb and forefinger. Wear surgical gloves or knock them off with a spray of water if you are squeamish.

Even when an insect infestation increases to such a level that it requires severer measures, the first line of attack should be a relatively nontoxic spray, such as horticultural soap or an ultrarefined, "summerweight" horticultural oil. In the Peggy Rockefeller Rose Garden even these sprays are rarely applied, because the roses are so healthy that they rarely experience any serious insect infestations.

In fact, during at least one recent growing season, Mike Ruggiero didn't spray for insects at all. Small outbreaks of aphids and Japanese beetles were easily controlled by nonchemical means. Of the Japanese beetles, he and the other gardeners counted a total of just 50 in the course of the entire season.

When problems do develop, early identification is the key to quick and easy treatment. At NYBG, insect and disease prevention starts early in the spring. As the gardeners remove the hills of earth from around the rosebushes' bases, they look for evidence of borers: dead canes with a hole in their tips (symptoms of this and other common pests and diseases will be found at this chapter's end). If borer damage is detected, the stem is cut open at the damaged site and visu-ally inspected for insects hiding in the pith. The gardeners continue to scrutinize the rosebushes—the stems, tops, and undersides of the leaves, and the new growth—throughout the growing season as they go about their other tasks. That is how they discovered an infestation of midges one season; they recognized the deformed flower buds as a symptom of that insect.

Ruggiero sprayed with an appropriate insecticide when he dis-covered the midge damage, because every flower bud counts in a public rose garden. In the home garden, though, your personal tol-erance may dictate a laxer policy—some gardeners don't mind rose-bushes with obvious evidence of insect damage. Others, such as those who raise roses for exhibition, demand pristine plants. So decide what your tolerance level is. And when that level is reached? "Spray." But be realistic. "If we all died tomorrow, the insects would be fine." One way or another, you must learn to coexist.

DISEASES

Whereas most gardeners are overzealous in their pursuit of "bugs," most are too lax in their treatment of rose diseases. In the Northeast, at least, diseases are the far more serious threat. Fungal diseases espe-cially afflict virtually all modern everblooming roses to some degree, and most of the old garden roses as well. Indeed, only *R. rugosa* and its hybrids can be described as anything like immune.

Fungal diseases. Mike Ruggiero sprays regularly for two fungal dis-eases: powdery mildew and blackspot. He generates a schedule detail-ing the necessary fungicidal treatments before the first bud breaks in the spring and keeps it on his computer so he can call it up as often as he needs it.

That is weekly. Ruggiero applies a fungicide every 7 to 10 days, or a total of about 20 times during the course of the growing season; Mondays, when the NYBG is closed to the public, are the usual days for spraying. He strives for consistency in this, for the consistency of the ap-plication is what determines a fungicide's effectiveness. This is because fungicides cannot cure a fungal infection; once the fungus has invaded a rose leaf or cane, the fungicide does not affect it. All that a fungicide can do is prevent the fungus from gaining entry, and for it to do that effectively, the fungicide must be present continuously. Missing a scheduled spray opens the door to infection, and leaving it open even briefly can lead to serious problems.

The reward for consistency is not only healthier roses, however. It can also be a healthier environment. Practice perfect consistency in your spraying, and you can control most fungal diseases satisfactorily with a homemade spray concocted of relatively harmless ingredients.

"If you start at leaf break," Ruggiero advises, "even if you don't spray toxic stuff, but you spray a formula of baking soda and oil, it works"—so long as you spray weekly and don't miss a single spray. This is not his discovery.

Decide what your tolerance level of insect damage is. And when that level is reached, spray.

The actual formula for the soda spray—3 teaspoons of baking soda and 2½ tablespoons of summer-weight horticultural oil mixed with a gallon of water—was developed by Dr. R.K. Horst of Cornell University's Department of Plant Pathology. It was Dr. Horst who discovered the spray's effectiveness in controlling powdery mildew and blackspot, too.

Ruggiero himself relies on more potent synthetic fungicides. Which ones? He won't make specific recommendations, because of the frequency with which the regulations governing chemicals change. Besides, the effectiveness of a given chemical seems to vary with the climate. For spray prescriptions, he sends gardeners to their local Cooperative Extension Service office (the telephone number is included in the county or state listings in the telephone book). The extension agent can tell you what's approved for your area, what's effective, and what's the safest spray for your environment, you, and the plant.

One thing Ruggiero is quite definite about is that not one but several different fungicides must be used and that their use must be rotated. Using the same fungicide time after time actually encourages the development and spread of strains of fungi resistant to that chemical. He remembers repeatedly applying Benomyl to the roses years ago, before he knew better. Overuse of any fungicide eventually renders it ineffective, much as overuse of particular antibiotics has destroyed their value.

As already noted, a rose garden's problem with diseases is largely due to the natural susceptibility of the plants. But problems with fungal infection are also due in part to the way in which, traditionally, we have grown roses.

Problems with roses planted together. A traditional rose garden, with the bushes massed together into beds, presents a large and vulnerable target to disease spores. These drift wherever the wind takes them and must rely on chance to find a suitable host; create a larger target, and the spore is much more likely to settle onto it. Initially, the disease will infect the more susceptible rose cultivars, but in a massed planting, it is almost sure to attack even resistant cultivars. The susceptible cultivars become a constant source of new spores, exposing neighbors to levels of these that even resistant cultivars cannot withstand. There is, how-

Precisely targeted sprays can reduce spraying to a minimum as well as reduce the hazard to wildlife. Always wear the protective gear recommended on the product label.

ever, an advantage to the traditional plantings: treatment of the diseases is easier, since all the roses can be sprayed at once.

Roses integrated with other plants. When roses are incorporated into mixed plantings, so that the bushes grow somewhat isolated from each other, then they are less likely to suffer from fungal infection—they present a smaller target, and resistant cultivars are more likely to fight off the disease successfully. Furthermore, if the disease should disfigure or even temporarily defoliate a rose, the visual impact is much less than if a whole bed is affected in this way. The disadvantage to mixed plantings is that monitoring the health of the roses and treating the fungal infections involves more effort.

In addition to careful garden design and choice of cultivars good gardening techniques also help a rose stay healthy. "Spores are in the air at all times," Ruggiero explains, "but if you plant three Hybrid Teas in your airiest location, with the best drainage, in the deepest soil, you'll probably be better off than someone who plants in a dark corner of the yard with no drainage and less soil." In other words, fungal diseases are symptoms of bad gardening.

Good gardening practice. The importance of adequate sunshine, deep soil, and good drainage is fairly obvious: these foster healthy roses that are better able to fight off diseases. An airy location is essential because the air currents there will carry off spores released from already infected foliage, so that fungal diseases won't spread as easily or as quickly. Proper pruning—giving the rosebushes an open, spreading structure and removing weak canes that choke the center of the bush—helps air pass through the plant.

Practicing good sanitation is also a key to reducing fungal disease problems. Fungi overwinter on canes and old leaves, waiting for the first spring rain to spread their spores back up into the air and onto your plants, and along with them may come insect pests that overwintered in the plant debris, too. Preventing this kind of reinfection begins with the fall pruning. At that time, cut off any weak or diseased canes in which the diseases may overwinter. Then rake or blow all the fallen leaves from around the rosebush. Bag and dispose of the leaves with the trash, or burn them; ordinary composting will not kill spores. Give the garden a good cleaning in early spring to remove any debris that may have escaped notice in the fall.

Weather also plays a role in disease control. As noted earlier, the gardener should keep watch for symptoms throughout the growing season, but this sort of vigilance is especially crucial during certain times of year and certain types of weather. In the spring and in fall, when cool nights follow warm days, powdery mildew flourishes. Later on in the season, as the summer heats up, blackspot becomes the main invader.

The threat posed by particular rose diseases also varies considerably with the geography. (For detailed information on regional distribution of rose diseases, see "The Best and the Worst" in the appendices.) Rust is a fungal disease that is prevalent in western gardens, for example; it is not a serious problem east of the Mississippi. Blackspot is most prevalent in areas with humid weather, such as summers in the Northeast. Yet even within that region there are differences. Blackspot isn't a serious problem, for instance, in gardens along the beaches of Long Island, New York. There sea breezes blow away the spores and keep the humidity down.

With diseases, as with so many other types of rose problems, the best protection is to plant the right roses. Plant cultivars or species that are naturally resistant, and nature will take care of most disease control for you. Ruggiero keeps notes on the disease susceptibility of every rose he tests (this information is included in the cultivar descriptions in the next chapter). If a rose proves susceptible even when treated with his schedule of sprays, it is ruthlessly culled.

A diagnostic guide. What follows is not a comprehensive guide to rose pests and diseases; they number in the hundreds. But the vast majority of these pests and diseases are seldom seen in home gardens or do not present a serious threat to the health of the rosebushes.

Instead, here are a baker's dozen of offenders that gardeners are almost certain to encounter if they make roses a part of their garden. Rather than specific recommendations about chemical sprays, there is information about alternative forms of effective treatment.

APHIDS

BLACKSPOT

These are the most common rose pest and, fortunately, one of the most easily controlled. Aphids are soft-bodied insects that suck sap from soft new growth and buds; if allowed to multiply unchecked, they may stunt or deform blossoms and leaves.

Treatment: If you manage your garden without the use of insecticides, natural predators such as ladybugs often provide adequate control of aphids. Alternatively, wash them off the rosebushes with a strong jet of water, or spray with insecticidal soaps. There are a number of approved insecticides, but the use of these is rarely necessary.

When round, fringed black spots appear on the leaves, this signals the fungal disease blackspot. Later the leaves turn yellow, spreading outward from the spots, and then they drop off the plant. If left to spread unchecked, blackspot may entirely defoliate a bush. Blackspot is especially common during humid or wet weather, and is worse with roses grown in less than ideal conditions, such as a too shady location. It is the most serious rose disease throughout the United States, with the exception only of the arid West and Southwest.

Treatment: Control by weekly sprays with an approved fungicide or with the homemade mixture of baking soda and summer-weight horticultural oil described earlier in this chapter. Good sanitation and cultivation also help with control. Gather and dispose of leaves that fall to the ground. (Don't infect the compost pile with them.)

BORERS

BOTRYTIS BLIGHT

If a rose cane dies back, check for a swollen band of tissue at the base of the dead wood and for a neat round hole in the cane's end. Both are signs that a borer—the larva of a bee, wasp, sawfly, or beetle—has tunneled into the cane. If you split the dead wood open with a sharp knife, you can trace the tunnel to the legless, cream-colored grub that hides at its bottom. Often the borer has taken advantage of a pruning wound to gain entry to the cane.

Treatment: When pruning, cover all cut ends with white glue. Cut back infested canes to a spot below the bottom of the borer's tunnel and dispose of the prunings.

Certain Hybrid Tea roses are especially prone to this fungal disease, which causes flower buds to turn brown and decay before they open.

Treatment: Winterkilled branches may harbor botrytis, so their prompt removal in spring is essential to the prevention of this disease. Likewise, infected blooms are a source of infection to other neighbors and should not be left to hang on the bush. Cultivars that prove particularly susceptible should be replaced; the schedule of fungicidal sprays designed for powdery mildew or blackspot will also control this disease.

CHEMICAL INJURY

CROWN GALL

There is a temptation to blame every kind of foliage damage on disease, but in many cases the remedy is what is causing the problem. Sudden discoloration or crisping of the leaves throughout the garden is probably due to a too generous application of chemicals or to spraying during very hot weather.

Treatment: There is no cure for this sort of damage; you must wait for the rosebushes to replace the damaged leaves. Prevent chemical injury by making sure of your diagnosis before you reach for the sprayer, and take special care with Rugosa roses, which cannot tolerate most fungicides and insecticides (and rarely need them anyway).

This soil-borne bacterial disease causes irregular masses of tissue to grow around the base of a rosebush's stems and the roots, particularly at the "crown," where stems and roots join.

Treatment: Plants infected with crown gall should be dug up and destroyed, and no other rose should be planted in that spot for at least two years. Commonly, this disease is introduced into the garden with infected stock shipped by a less than scrupulous nursery. Make sure that any plants you buy are certified disease-free.

JAPANESE BEETLES

Their visibility makes these insects an especially offensive pest, together with their preference for buds and blossoms. They also feed on leaf tissues, reducing leaves to characteristically "skeletonized" networks of veins.

The beautiful metallic green and copper-colored adult beetles begin appearing in late June and increase in numbers into July, then gradually disappear in August. During their active period, the females lay eggs in the ground—they favor the relatively soft, moist soil of well-irrigated lawns—which develop into dirty white grubs with brown heads. These overwinter deep in the soil and then gradually work their way upward to emerge as the next year's crop of beetles.

Treatment: Because these beetles are strong fliers and continually reinvade treated areas, sprays do not provide control unless they are applied often enough to keep the buds and foliage continually coated with toxins.

If you grow old garden roses, they'll finish their season of bloom before the adult beetles appear in substantial numbers, so that the flowers will not be eaten. And nipping off the flower buds from modern roses through July will reduce the number of beetles attracted to your garden and may encourage early arrivals to move on. Your bushes will produce a fine flush of flowers in the fall.

Discouraging the adults is important because Japanese beetles lay their eggs in and around the food source. Handpicking adults from your roses will have a significant impact: every mating pair you drop in a jar full of soapy water may mean 100 less grubs the following season. Leaving your lawn unirrigated through the summer will have a substantial effect on the beetle population there—the beetles are likely to fly away and lay their eggs in the perfect green carpet of the amateur greenskeeper down the street.

MIDGES

POWDERY MILDEW

There are a number of causes for what rosarians call "blind wood," shoots that fail to produce flowers buds at their tips. If buds do develop on other canes but grow in a stunted, twisted manner you can be sure the cause is an infestation of midges.

These are small, yellow-brown flies that lay their eggs in rose flower and leaf buds. The maggots that hatch from the eggs feed on the plant tissues, and this may cause the buds to abort entirely or to grow in this characteristically distorted pattern.

Treatment: Pruning off and burning or otherwise disposing of the infested canes will help control this insect, but usually an application of an approved insecticide is also necessary.

Warm days followed by cool nights commonly trigger this disease. A white, powdery growth appears on young leaves and spreads over whole shoots, stunting new growth and deforming or aborting flowers.

This disease is pervasive in the desert Southwest and in southern California, and in the North it is common at certain times of year, especially early fall. It is particularly rampant in enclosed, poorly aerated plantings and is also promoted by too generous applications of nitrogen fertilizers.

Treatment: Remove infected leaves, and increase aeration by pruning roses to a more open form or by transplanting to a more open spot. Spray with an approved fungicide or with the baking soda/horticultural oil mixture described earlier in this chapter.

SCALE

SPIDER MITES

This insect pest looks just like the name suggests, and it forms encrustation on shoots and leaves; heavy infestations can look like a coat of whitewash. Scale insects suck plant juices, causing stunting and discoloration.

Treatment: Heavily infested canes should be pruned away. Spray bushes with dormant oil in early spring before bud break, or with an approved insecticide when eggs hatch and small, legged "crawlers" emerge, in late spring and again in midsummer in the North.

Mites, tiny relatives of the spider, are practically invisible to the naked eye, but the damage they do is obvious and easily recognized. These red, eight-legged creatures pierce the rose leaves from the underside and suck the sap, causing the foliage to turn gray, yellow, or even reddish. A fine cobweb is a symptom of a heavy infestation, which can stunt new growth and cause leaves to drop prematurely.

Treatment: An open, airy site is a good preventive, since mites flourish in crowded, stagnant gardens. Early in the day, so the moisture has the opportunity to evaporate, spray infested bushes with water, taking care to hit the undersides of the leaves. If the infestation persists, apply a recommended miticide.

STEM CANKER

THRIPS

If shoots wilt suddenly, check the cane for red to purple lesions. These are symptoms of stem canker, a fungal disease that gains entry to the living tissue through any sort of wound to the bark: pruning cuts, insect damage, and the like.

Treatment: If signs of canker are found, prune off the diseased cane, cutting well below the infected area. To prevent infection, avoid making any cuts during wet weather; persistent cases may require treatment with an approved fungicide.

Deformed flowers with flecked petals are one signature of this pest; sometimes a bud will color and swell, sometimes it will open partway into a ball of brown-edged petals. All of these symptoms are caused by the rasping mouthparts of thrips, which injure plant tissues so that they can drink the sap. Some thrips also attack leaves, leaving them tan and dry.

Though the damage thrips cause is immediately apparent, the feathery-winged small brown insect is not; it commonly hides inside the blossoms, which must be pulled apart to expose the culprit.

Treatment: Dusting plants with diatomaceous earth provides some control; persistent infestations should be sprayed with an approved insecticide. Thrips are especially attracted to yellow roses.

Rosa Pimpinelli-folia inermis.   *Rosier Pimprenelle à tiges sans é*

P. J. Redouté pinx.   Imprimerie de Remond.   Lange

7
RECOMMENDED ROSES

When he is asked to list 80 of his favorite roses, Mike Ruggiero's response is a simple no. The roses that he favors, he explains, vary with the circumstances: the best rose is the rose that has been chosen to suit its site, exposure, climate, and the needs of the garden's design. In addition, Ruggiero believes that a list of his favorites is of little value to another gardener with different tastes.

The list of 80 roses that follows is really a summation of Ruggiero's computer file of cultivars that have consistently given the best performance at The New York Botanical Garden over several years. All have proved winter-hardy when given the protection of a hill of soil and compost around their bases; all have proved acceptably resistant to fungal diseases when given the protection of a regular schedule of sprays. None will perform well in every situation, but most gardeners, except for those in the Deep South, will find roses here that will prove rewarding and reliable in their own gardens.

A photographic portrait has been included with each of the following rose profiles, and whenever possible a view has been selected that illustrates the character of the bush as a whole and especially the way in which the flowers are borne—singly, in sprays, or in masses. But though the pictures tell much, gardeners will also find invaluable, and uncommon, information in the accompanying text.

Hybridization history. Included in the profiles are the names of the roses from which each cultivar was bred and the name of the hybridizer. Performance is largely determined by descent; if a gardener has found the Hybrid Tea 'Fragrant Cloud' a reliable rose in his or her garden, then he or she should consider a trial of its offspring, 'Folklore'. Likewise, if the Floribunda 'Iceberg' has proved satisfactory, a gardener ought to investigate its parent, the Hybrid

Reliability commonly runs in the family—if the wonderfully perfumed Hybrid Tea 'Fragrant Cloud' (above) has performed well in your garden, chances are that its offspring, the orange-blossomed 'Folklore', will thrive there, too.

Musk rose 'Robin Hood', and perhaps the other Hybrid Musks as well.

The name of the hybridizer is significant because each rose cultivar reflects not only descent but also the vision of the person who bred it. If 'Gene Boerner' appeals to you, then certainly you should investigate the 180-odd other roses the hybridizer, Mr. Boerner himself, produced; in this way you may discover classics such as the pink-flowered Floribunda 'Fashion' and the white-flowered Hybrid Tea 'John F. Kennedy'.

Indivdual characteristics. The main body of each rose profile is a detailed description of the features that make each plant distinctive and determine its use in the garden. Of special interest to contemporary gardeners will be the descriptions of the mature foliage and the new growth—as the rose integrates back into the garden, a cultivar's value as a foliage plant takes on new importance. The vivid red new growth of the Grandiflora rose 'Love', for example, will give it a bold presence in spring that differs dramatically from the Shrub rose 'Robusta', whose new growth is a more sober green.

Prizes and awards. A list of the prizes that each rose has won is included because these indicate a favorable judgment by the world's foremost rosarians. A particular rose's failure to receive recognition of this kind, however, should not discourage readers from trying it in their gardens, since to a large extent, a cultivar's performance will depend on the conditions it finds in *your* garden; a rose that

> *The best rose is the rose that has been chosen to suit its site, exposure, and climate, and the needs of the garden's design.*

was a first-prize winner in the All-America Rose Selection trial gardens may come in second in yours. Keep in mind, too, that all the roses included here are exceptional plants.

These rose profiles are a beginning—serious gardeners will use them as a guide and a starting point for their own exploration of the genus *Rosa*'s endless diversity. But the profiles are also a summation, a distillation of years of observations. From them, beginning rosarians may learn not only where to look for quality but also what to look for.

'CHRYSLER IMPERIAL'	**'FOLKLORE'**	**'IVORY TOWER'**
('Charlotte Armstrong' × *'Mirandy') 1952*	*('Fragrant Cloud' × seedling)* *1977*	*('Colour Wonder' × 'King's* *Ransom') 1979*
Hybridizer: *Dr. W.E. Lammerts, Germain Seed & Plant Co., Los Angeles, Calif.*	**Hybridizer:** *Barni Kordes, Germany*	**Hybridizer:** *Reimer Kordes, Germany; introduced by Armstrong Nursery, Ontario, Calif.*
Buds: *long, pointed* **Flowers:** *deep red, double (45 petals), 4–4.5" wide*	**Buds:** *long, pointed* **Flowers:** *orange with reverse petals lighter, double (44 petals)*	**Buds:** *long, pointed* **Flowers:** *ivory white shaded light pink and light yellow, double (35 petals), 5–5.5" wide*
Fragrance: *very strong*	**Fragrance:** *mild to light*	**Fragrance:** *mild to light*
Foliage: *dark green, semiglossy; new growth light to medium red* **Height:** *average upright growth*	**Foliage:** *medium green, glossy; new growth medium red* **Height:** *very tall, upright, bushy growth*	**Foliage:** *medium green; new growth medium red* **Height:** *tall, upright, bushy growth*
Disease resistance: *good*	**Disease resistance:** *superior*	**Disease resistance:** *superior*
Awards: *All-America Rose Selection 1953 Gold Medal Portland 1951 American Rose National Gold Medal 1956 James Alexander Gamble Rose Fragrance Medal 1965*		

'JARDINS DE BAGATELLE' (*'Queen Elizabeth' × 'Eleg' × 'Meldraglac'*) 1986	**'OLYMPIAD'** (*'Red Planet' × 'Pharaoh'*) 1982	**'PARADISE'** (*'Swarthmore' × seedling*) 1978
Hybridizer: *Marie-Louise Meilland, Meilland Roses, France*	**Hybridizer:** *Sam McGredy, New Zealand; introduced by Armstrong Nursery, Ontario, Calif.*	**Hybridizer:** *Weeks, Conard Pyle Co., West Grove, Pa.*
Buds: *long, pointed* **Flowers:** *white with pale pink shades maturing pure white, double (40+ petals)*	**Buds:** *short, pointed* **Flowers:** *brilliant medium red, double (35 petals), 4.5–5" wide*	**Buds:** *long, pointed* **Flowers:** *silvery lavender shading to ruby red at edge, double (28 petals), 3.5–4.5" wide*
Fragrance: *very strong*	**Fragrance:** *mild*	**Fragrance:** *strong*
Foliage: *large, medium green to blue-green, semiglossy; new growth light red* **Height:** *low to medium 3–3.5' bushy growth*	**Foliage:** *medium green; new growth medium red* **Height:** *tall, upright, narrow growth*	**Foliage:** *glossy dark green; new growth dark red* **Height:** *medium, upright growth*
Disease resistance: *superior*	**Disease resistance:** *good*	**Disease resistance:** *superior*
Awards: *Gold Medal Genoa (Italy) 1987*	**Awards:** *All-America Rose Selection 1984 Gold Medal Portland 1985*	**Awards:** *All-America Rose Selection 1979 Gold Medal Portland 1979*

'PEACE' (['George Dickson' × 'Souvenir de Claudius Pernet'] × ['Joanna Hill' × 'Charles P. Kilham'] × 'Margaret McGredy') 1945	**'PERFECT MOMENT'** ('New Day' × seedling) 1989	**'PINK PEACE'** (['Peace' × 'Monique'] × ['Peace' × 'Mrs. John Laing']) 1959
Hybridizer: Francis Meilland, France; introduced by Conard Pyle Co., West Grove, Pa.	**Hybridizer:** Wilhelm Sohne Kordes, Germany; introduced by Bear Creek Gardens Inc.	**Hybridizer:** Francis Meilland, France; Universal Rose Selection, Conard Pyle Co., West Grove, Pa.
Buds: high-centered to cupped **Flowers:** golden yellow edged rose-pink, double (45 petals), large 6"	**Buds:** pointed, open cupped **Flowers:** red on outer half of petal, yellow on inner, reverse yellow with red blush, double (30+ petals)	**Buds:** long, pointed **Flowers:** deep pink, double (58 petals), 6" wide
Fragrance: mild	**Fragrance:** mild	**Fragrance:** very strong
Foliage: large, leathery, glossy; new growth light red **Height:** medium, bushy growth	**Foliage:** semiglossy; new growth medium red **Height:** medium, upright, bushy growth	**Foliage:** large, leathery, glossy; new growth light red **Height:** medium, upright, vigorous growth
Disease resistance: good	**Disease resistance:** good	**Disease resistance:** superior
Awards: Gold Medal Portland 1944 All-America Rose Selection 1946 ARS National Gold Medal 1947 Golden Rose of The Hague 1965	**Awards:** All-America Rose Selection 1991	**Awards:** Gold Medal Geneva 1959 Gold Medal Rome 1959

'PRECIOUS PLATINUM' (*'Red Planet'* × *'Franklin Englemann'*) 1974	**'TIFFANY'** (*'Charlotte Armstrong'* × *'Girona'*) 1954	**'TOUCH OF CLASS'** (*'Micaëla'* × *'Queen Elizabeth'* × *'Romantica'*) 1986
Hybridizer: *Dicksons of Hawlmark, Northern Ireland*	**Hybridizer:** *Robert V. Lindquist, Howard Rose Co., Helmet, Calif.*	**Hybridizer:** *Michel Kriloff, France; introduced by Armstrong Nursery, Ontario, Calif.*
Buds: *ovoid* **Flowers:** *cardinal red, double (50+ petals), high-centered, 4–5" wide*	**Buds:** *long, pointed* **Flowers:** *pink-yellow blend, double (28 petals), high-centered, 4–5" wide*	**Buds:** *short, pointed* **Flowers:** *medium pink, shaded coral and orange, double (33 petals), 4–4.5" wide*
Fragrance: *mild*	**Fragrance:** *very strong*	**Fragrance:** *mild*
Foliage: *dark glossy green; new growth deep red* **Height:** *medium to high, vigorous, bushy growth*	**Foliage:** *dark green; new growth medium red* **Height:** *upright growth*	**Foliage:** *dark green, semiglossy; new growth medium red* **Height:** *medium to tall, upright, vigorous growth*
Disease resistance: *superior*	**Disease resistance:** *good*	**Disease resistance:** *superior*
	Awards: *Gold Medal Portland 1954* *All-America Rose Selection 1955* *ARS Davis Fuerstenberg Prize 1957* *James Alexander Gamble Rose Fragrance Medal 1962*	**Awards:** *All-America Rose Selection 1986* *Gold Medal Portland 1988*

'YVES PIAGET' *(['Pharaoh' × 'Peace'] × ['Chrysler Imperial' × 'Charles Mallerin'] × 'Tamanger') 1985*	**'PINK PARFAIT'** *('First Love' × 'Pinocchio') 1960*	**'LOVE'** *(seedling × 'Redgold') 1980*
Hybridizer: *Marie-Louise Meilland, Et Cie France*	**Hybridizer:** *Herbert Swim, Armstrong Nursery, Ontario, Calif.*	**Hybridizer:** *William A. Warriner, Jackson & Perkins, Medford, Ore.*
Buds: *ovoid* **Flowers:** *deep pink, double (40+ petals), 5.5" wide*	**Buds:** *ovoid to urn-shaped* **Flowers:** *outer petals medium pink, center blended pale orange, double (23 petals), 3.5–4" wide*	**Buds:** *short, pointed* **Flowers:** *petals bright red, reverse silvery white, double (35 petals), 3.5" wide*
Fragrance: *very strong*	**Fragrance:** *mild*	**Fragrance:** *slight*
Foliage: *medium dark green, semiglossy; new growth medium red* **Height:** *medium, upright growth*	**Foliage:** *medium to dark green, semiglossy; new growth medium red* **Height:** *medium, bushy growth*	**Foliage:** *dark green; new growth dark red* **Height:** *medium, upright, bushy growth*
Disease resistance: *good*	**Disease resistance:** *good*	**Disease resistance:** *superior*
	Awards: *Gold Medal Baden-Baden 1959* *Gold Medal Portland 1959* *All-America Rose Selection 1961* *Gold Medal Royal National Rose Society 1962*	**Awards:** *All-America Rose Selection 1980* *Gold Medal Portland 1980*

'QUEEN ELIZABETH'
(*'Charlotte Armstrong'* ×
'Floradora') 1954

'TOURNAMENT OF ROSES'
(*'Impatient'* × *seedling*) 1988

'BETTY PRIOR'
(*'Kirsten Poulsen'* × *seedling*)
1935

Hybridizer: *Dr. W.E. Lammerts,
Germain Seed & Plant Co.,
Los Angeles, Calif.*

Hybridizer: *William A. Warriner,
Jackson & Perkins,
Medford, Ore.*

Hybridizer: *Prior, introduced
by Jackson & Perkins,
Medford, Ore.*

Buds: *pointed*
Flowers: *medium pink,
high-centered to cupped,
double (38 petals), 3.5–4" wide,
borne singly or in clusters*

Buds: *ovoid*
Flowers: *light coral, reverse deep
pink aging coral, double (40+
petals), high-centered, 3–4" wide,
borne singly or in sprays*

Buds: *ovoid, dark carmine*
Flowers: *carmine-pink, lighter
in warm weather; single
(5 petals), in clusters*

Fragrance: *little or none*

Fragrance: *little or none*

Fragrance: *little or none*

Foliage: *dark green, glossy;
new growth medium green*
Height: *tall, vigorous growth*

Foliage: *dark green, semiglossy;
new growth medium red, glossy*
Height: *medium, upright,
bushy growth*

Foliage: *medium green,
semiglossy; new growth
medium red, semiglossy*
Height: *medium,
upright growth*

Disease resistance: *superior*

Disease resistance: *good*

Disease resistance: *superior*

Awards: *Gold Medal Portland
1954; Gold Medal Royal National
Rose Society 1955; All-America
Rose Selection 1955; Presidents
International Trophy (England)
1955; ARS Gertrude M. Hubbard
Gold Medal 1957*

Awards: *All-America Rose
Selection 1989*

Awards: *Gold Medal Royal
National Rose Society 1933*

159

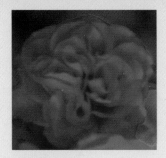

'ESCAPADE' ('Pink Parfait' × 'Baby Faurax') 1967	**'EUROPEANA'** ('Ruth Leuwerik' × 'Rosemary Rose') 1963	**'FRENSHAM'** (Floribunda seedling × 'Crimson Glory') 1946
Hybridizer: R. Harkness, Harkness Rose Co., Hitchin, Hertfordshire, England	**Hybridizer:** George de Ruiter, Holland; introduced by Conard Pyle Co., West Grove, Pa.	**Hybridizer:** Norman A.Harkness, Harkness Rose Co., Surrey, England; introduced by Conard Pyle Co., West Grove, Pa.
Buds: short, pointed **Flowers:** magenta-rose, centered white, semidouble (12 petals), 3" wide, in slightly fragrant clusters	**Buds:** ovoid **Flowers:** dark crimson, double (30+ petals), 3" wide, blooms in heavy clusters	**Buds:** short, pointed **Flowers:** deep scarlet, semidouble (15 petals), medium-size, borne in clusters
Fragrance: moderate	**Fragrance:** mild	**Fragrance:** mild
Foliage: light green, new growth green tinged red **Height:** tall, upright, bushy growth	**Foliage:** dark green, leathery; new growth deep red **Height:** medium, vigorous, bushy growth	**Foliage:** medium green, semiglossy; new growth green tinged red, glossy **Height:** medium, bushy, vigorous growth
Disease resistance: superior	**Disease resistance:** good	**Disease resistance:** superior
Awards: Gold Medal Belfast 1959 Gold Medal Baden-Baden 1959 Anerkannte Deutsche Rose 1973	**Awards:** Gold Medal The Hague 1962 All-America Rose Selection 1968 Gold Medal Portland 1970	**Awards:** Gold Medal Royal National Rose Society 1943 Anerkannte Deutsche Rose 1955

		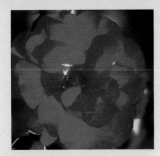
'GENE BOERNER' ('Ma Perkins' × 'Garnette Supreme') 1968	**'ICEBERG'** ('Robin Hood' × 'Virgo') 1958	**'LILLI MARLEEN'** (['Our Princess' × 'Rudolph Timm'] × 'Ama') 1959
Hybridizer: Eugene S. Boerner, Jackson & Perkins, Medford, Ore.	**Hybridizer:** Reimer Kordes, Germany	**Hybridizer:** Reimer Kordes, Germany; introduced by McGredy Roses International 1959 and Jackson & Perkins 1961
Buds: ovoid **Flowers:** deep pink, double (35 petals), high-centered, 3" wide	**Buds:** long, pointed **Flowers:** pure white, double (30+ petals), in clusters	**Buds:** ovoid **Flowers:** medium to scarlet red, double (25 petals), 3" wide, cupped
Fragrance: mild	**Fragrance:** mild to strong	**Fragrance:** little to none
Foliage: dark green, glossy; new growth medium red **Height:** medium, upright, vigorous growth	**Foliage:** light green, glossy; new growth green tinged red, glossy **Height:** medium, upright, bushy, vigorous growth	**Foliage:** dark green, leathery; new growth medium red, semiglossy **Height:** medium, vigorous, bushy growth
Disease resistance: superior	**Disease resistance:** good	**Disease resistance:** good
Awards: All-America Rose Selection 1969	**Awards:** Gold Medal Royal National Rose Society 1958 Gold Medal Baden-Baden 1958	**Awards:** Anerkannte Deutsche Rose 1960 Golden Rose of The Hague 1966

'MARGARET MERRIL'
('Rudolph Timm'× ['Dedication'
× 'Pascali'] 1977

'SUNSPRITE'
(seedling× 'Spanish Sun') 1977

'TRUMPETER'
('Satchmo'× seedling) 1977

Hybridizer: *R. Harkness, Harkness Rose Co., Hitchen, Hertfordshire, England*

Hybridizer: *Reimer Kordes, Germany; introduced by Jackson & Perkins, Medford, Ore.*

Hybridizer: *Sam McGredy, McGredy Roses International, Auckland, New Zealand*

Buds: *short, pointed*
Flowers: *blush-white, double (28 petals), high-centered, 4" wide*

Buds: *ovoid*
Flowers: *deep yellow, double (28 petals), 3" wide*

Buds: *ovoid*
Flowers: *orange-red, double (39 petals), 3.5" wide, cupped*

Fragrance: *very fragrant*

Fragrance: *strong*

Fragrance: *mild*

Foliage: *light green, semiglossy; new growth light red, semiglossy*
Height: *medium, busy growth*

Foliage: *light to medium green, glossy; new growth light red*
Height: *medium, upright, bushy growth*

Foliage: *medium green, glossy; new growth medium red, glossy*
Height: *compact, bushy growth*

Disease resistance: *good*

Disease resistance: *good*

Disease resistance: *superior*

Awards: *Gold Medal Geneva 1978*
Gold Medal Monza Rome 1978
Royal National Rose Society James Mason Gold Medal 1990

Awards: *Gold Medal Baden-Baden 1972*

Awards: *Gold Medal New Zealand 1977*
Gold Medal Portland 1981
Royal National Rose Society James Mason Medal 1991

'BONICA' (*'Meidomanac'*) (*[R. sempervirens × 'Mlle Marthe Carron']× 'Picasso'*) 1981	**'CAREFREE WONDER'** (*['Prairie Princess' × 'Nirvana'] × ['Eyepaint' × 'Rustica']*) 1978	**'PINK MEIDILAND'** (*'Anne de Bretagne' × 'Nirvana'*) 1984
Hybridizer: *Marie-Louise Meilland, France; introduced by Conard Pyle Co., West Grove, Pa.*	**Hybridizer:** *Meilland, France; introduced by Conard Pyle Co., West Grove, Pa.*	**Hybridizer:** *Marie-Louise Meilland, Meilland & Sons, France*
Buds: *ovoid* **Flowers:** *medium pink with lighter pink on edges, double (40+ petals), recurrent*	**Buds:** *pointed* **Flowers:** *medium pink with light pink reverse aging to medium pink, double (26 petals), 3.5" wide, cupped and borne in sprays of 1–4, recurrent*	**Buds:** *short, pointed* **Flowers:** *deep pink with a white eye, single (5 petals), medium in size, recurrent*
Fragrance: *little to none*	**Fragrance:** *little to none*	**Fragrance:** *none*
Foliage: *small, semiglossy, dark green; new growth green edged with red, glossy* **Height:** *medium, bushy growth*	**Foliage:** *medium green, semiglossy; new growth light red* **Height:** *bushy, upright growth, suitable for hedges*	**Foliage:** *small, medium green, semiglossy; new growth light to medium red* **Height:** *upright, tall, bushy growth, suitable for hedges*
Disease resistance: *good*	**Disease resistance:** *superior*	**Disease resistance:** *good*
Awards: *Anerkannte Deutsche Rose 1983 All-America Rose Selection 1987*	**Awards:** *All-America Rose Selection 1991*	**Awards:** *Anerkannte Deutsche Rose 1987*

'ROBUSTA'
(seedling × R. rugosa) 1979

'BLAZE IMPROVED'
*—Large-flowered climber
('Paul's Scarlet Climber' ×
'Gruss an Teplitz') 1932*

'CLAIR MATIN'—*Large-
flowered climber ('Fashion' ×
['Independence' × 'Orange
Triumph']× 'Phyllis Bide') 1960*

Hybridizer: *Wilhelm Sohne Kordes, Germany*	**Hybridizer:** *Joseph W. Callay, Jackson & Perkins, Medford, Ore.*	**Hybridizer:** *Marie-Louise Meilland, Universal Rose Selection; introduced by Conard Pyle Co., West Grove, Pa.*
Buds: *long, pointed* **Flowers:** *medium red, single (5 petals), 2.5" wide, recurrent*	**Buds:** *pointed* **Flowers:** *bright scarlet, semidouble (20 petals), cupped, 2–3" wide, in large clusters, recurrent*	**Buds:** *pointed* **Flowers:** *pink, semidouble (15 petals), cupped to flat, 3" wide, borne in clusters, recurrent*
Fragrance: *mild to strong*	**Fragrance:** *little to none*	**Fragrance:** *mild to strong*
Foliage: *dark green, glossy, leathery; new growth green, semiglossy* **Height:** *tall, vigorous, upright, bushy growth*	**Foliage:** *medium green, leathery, vigorous; new growth green tinged red* **Height:** *6–8"*	**Foliage:** *medium green, leathery, vigorous; new growth medium red, semiglossy* **Height:** *10–12'*
Disease resistance: *good*	**Disease resistance:** *good*	**Disease resistance:** *good*
Awards: *Anerkannte Deutsche Rose 1980*		**Awards:** *Gold Medal Bagatelle 1960*

'CLIMBING ICEBERG' —*Climbing Floribunda (sport of 'Iceberg') 1968*	**'DORTMUND'** —*Kordesii shrub used as climber (seedling × R. kordesii) 1955*	**'GOLDEN SHOWERS'** —*Large-flowered climber ('Charlotte Armstrong' × 'Captain Thomas') 1956*
Selected by *B.R. Cant, England*	**Hybridizer:** *Kordes, Germany*	**Hybridizer:** *Dr. W.E. Lammerts, Germain Seed & Plant Co., Los Angeles, Calif.*
Flowers: *Same as Floribunda 'Iceberg', recurrent*	**Buds:** *long, pointed* **Flowers:** *red with white eye, single (5 petals), 3.5–4" wide, in clusters, recurrent*	**Buds:** *long, pointed* **Flowers:** *daffodil yellow, double (27 petals), high-centered to flat, 4" wide, singly or in clusters, recurrent*
Fragrance: *mild*	**Fragrance:** *mild*	**Fragrance:** *strong*
Foliage: *Same as Floribunda 'Iceberg'* **Height:** *12–14'*	**Foliage:** *dark green, very glossy and vigorous; new growth green and glossy* **Height:** *10–12'*	**Foliage:** *dark green, glossy, vigorous; new growth light red, glossy* **Height:** *6–10'*
Disease resistance: *good*	**Disease resistance:** *good*	**Disease resistance:** *good*
	Awards: *Anerkannte Deutsche Rose 1954 Gold Medal Portland 1971*	**Awards:** *Gold Medal Portland 1957 All-America Rose Selection 1957*

'GOLDSTERN'
('Goldstar')—*Kordesii shrub used as climber 1961*

'HAMBURGER PHOENIX'
—*Kordesii shrub used as climber*
(R. kordesii × seedling) 1957

'ILLUSION'
—*Kordesii shrub used as climber 1961*

Hybridizer: *Math. Tandau, Germany*	**Hybridizer:** *Kordes, Germany*	**Hybridizer:** *Reimer Kordes, Germany*
Buds: *long, pointed* **Flowers:** *golden yellow, double (25 petals), 4" wide, in clusters, recurrent*	**Buds:** *long, pointed* **Flowers:** *rich red, semidouble (12–15 petals) 4" wide, in clusters, recurrent*	**Buds:** *long, pointed* **Flowers:** *bloodred to cinnabar, double (30+ petals), recurrent*
Fragrance: *mild to strong*	**Fragrance:** *slight*	**Fragrance:** *strong*
Foliage: *medium green, glossy; new growth light green edged with red* **Height:** *7–8', bushy growth*	**Foliage:** *dark green, very glossy, vigorous; new growth medium red, glossy* **Height:** *to 8'*	**Foliage:** *light green, leathery, glossy, vigorous; new growth green, glossy* **Height:** *12–14'*
Disease resistance: *good*	**Disease resistance:** *good*	**Disease resistance:** *good*

'JOHN CABOT' —*Kordesii shrub used as climber* (R. kordesii × seedling) 1978	**'MAY QUEEN'** —*Rambler* (R. wichuraiana × 'Champion of the World') 1898	**'NEW DAWN'** —*Large-flowered climber* ('Dr. W. Van Fleet' sport) 1930
Hybridizer: *Dr. Felicitas J. Svejda, Canada Dept. of Agriculture, Ontario, Canada*	**Hybridizer:** *W.A. Manda, South Orange, N.J.*	**Selected by** *Somerset Rose Nursery*
Buds: *ovoid* **Flowers:** *medium red, double (40 petals), 2.5" wide, in clusters, recurrent*	**Buds:** *pointed* **Flowers:** *clear pink, very double (45–55 petals), 3.25" wide, nonrecurrent*	**Buds:** *pointed* **Flowers:** *cameo pink fading to white, double (35–40 petals), 2.5–3.5" wide, slightly recurrent*
Fragrance: *strong*	**Fragrance:** *mild*	**Fragrance:** *mild*
Foliage: *yellow-green, semiglossy; new growth light red, glossy* **Height:** *to 8', upright, vigorous growth*	**Foliage:** *dark green, new growth green and glossy* **Height:** *to 20', vigorous growth*	**Foliage:** *dark green, very glossy; new growth green, glossy* **Height:** *15–20', very vigorous growth*
Disease resistance: *good*	**Disease resistance:** *good*	**Disease resistance:** *good*

'TRIER' —*Hybrid Multiflora (probably 'Aglaia' self-seedling) 1904*	**'VEILCHENBLAU'** —*Hybrid Multiflora ('Crimson Rambler' × 'Erinnerung an Brod') 1909*	**'WILLIAM BAFFIN'** —*Kordesii shrub used as climber (R. kordesii × seedling) 1983*
Selected by *P. Lambert, Trier, Germany*	**Hybridizer:** *J.C. Schmidt, Erfurt, Germany*	**Hybridizer:** *Dr. Felicitas J. Svejda, Canada Dept. of Agriculture, Ontario, Canada*
Buds: *ovoid* **Flowers:** *white with a slight rosy tint, base straw yellow, semidouble (8–10 petals), large clusters, nonrecurrent*	**Buds:** *ovoid* **Flowers:** *violet streaked white, semidouble (12+ petals), small, 1.25" wide, cupped with white anthers, in large clusters on short stems, nonrecurrent*	**Buds:** *ovoid* **Flowers:** *deep pink, double (20 petals), cupped, 2–3" wide, in large clusters, recurrent*
Fragrance: *mild to strong*	**Fragrance:** *mild*	**Fragrance:** *mild*
Foliage: *small, medium green, semiglossy; new growth green, glossy* **Height:** *6–8'*	**Foliage:** *large, pointed, glossy with very few prickles; new growth light green* **Height:** *10–15', vigorous growth*	**Foliage:** *dark green, glossy* **Height:** *10–12', very vigorous growth*
Disease resistance: *good*	**Disease resistance:** *good*	**Disease resistance:** *good*

'CANDY SUNBLAZE'	**'MAGIC CARROUSEL'**	**'PRIDE 'N' JOY'**
(*'Lady Sunblaze' sport*) 1991	(*'Little Darling'* × *'Westmont'*) 1972	(*'Chattem Centennial'* × *'Prominent'*) 1991
Hybridizer: *Meilland Selection; introduced by Conard Pyle Co., West Grove, Pa.*	**Hybridizer:** *Ralph S. Moore, Sequoia Nursery, Visalia, Calif.*	**Hybridizer:** *William A. Warriner, Bear Creek Gardens Inc.*
Buds: *ovoid* **Flowers:** *deep pink, very double (40+ petals), 1.5–2" wide*	**Buds:** *ovoid* **Flowers:** *petals white edged red, double (30–35 petals), 1–1.5" wide, high-centered*	**Buds:** *ovoid* **Flowers:** *bright medium orange, reverse orange and cream fading to salmon-pink, double (30–35 petals), 1–1.5" wide, urn-shaped*
Fragrance: *mild*	**Fragrance:** *slight*	**Fragrance:** *mild*
Foliage: *dark green, glossy; new growth deep red, glossy* **Height:** *upright, bushy growth*	**Foliage:** *small, dark green, semiglossy, leathery; new growth green tinged red* **Height:** *bushy, vigorous growth*	**Foliage:** *dark green; new growth medium red* **Height:** *bushy, spreading growth*
Disease resistance: *good*	**Disease resistance:** *good*	**Disease resistance:** *good*
	Awards: *Award of Excellence (for Miniatures) 1975*	**Awards:** *All-America Rose Selection 1992*

ENGLISH ROSES

'SCARLET SUNBLAZE' (*'Tamango'* × *['Baby Betina'* × *'Duchess of Windsor']*) 1982	**'ABRAHAM DARBY'** —Shrub (*'Yellow Cushion'* × *'Aloha'*) 1985	**'EVELYN'** —Shrub (*'Graham Thomas'* × *'Austamora'*) 1991
Hybridizer: *Marie-Louise Meilland, France; introduced by Conard Pyle Co., West Grove, Pa.*	**Hybridizer:** *David Austin, Austin Roses, Albrighton, England*	**Hybridizer:** *David Austin, Austin Roses, Albrighton, England*
Buds: *ovoid* **Flowers:** *dark red, semidouble (20 petals), 1.5–2" wide*	**Buds:** *pointed* **Flowers:** *peach blend inside with pale yellow reverse, opens apricot-yellow, very double (60+ petals), 3.5–4" wide, singly and in clusters, recurrent*	**Buds:** *pointed* **Flowers:** *apricot, rosette form, double (45+ petals), 3.5–4" wide, in small clusters, recurrent*
Fragrance: *little to none*	**Fragrance:** *strong*	**Fragrance:** *very strong*
Foliage: *dark green, dull; new growth green-red* **Height:** *low, bushy growth*	**Foliage:** *dark green, glossy; new growth medium red* **Height:** *5' as shrub or 8–10' as climber*	**Foliage:** *medium green, semiglossy; new growth medium red, semiglossy* **Height:** *4–5' upright, bushy growth*
Disease resistance: *good*	**Disease resistance:** *good*	**Disease resistance:** *good*

'GERTRUDE JEKYLL' —*Shrub ('Wife of Bath' ×* *'Comte de Chambord') 1986*	**'GRAHAM THOMAS'** —*Shrub ('Charles Austin' ×* *'Iceberg' seedling) 1983*	**'LILIAN AUSTIN'** —*Shrub ('Aloha' ×* *'The Yeoman') 1973*
Hybridizer: *David Austin,* *Austin Roses, Albrighton,* *England*	**Hybridizer:** *David Austin,* *Austin Roses, Albrighton,* *England*	**Hybridizer:** *David Austin,* *Austin Roses, Albrighton,* *England*
Buds: *pointed* **Flowers:** *deep pink,* *very double (50+ petals),* *4" wide, recurrent*	**Buds:** *pointed* **Flowers:** *deep yellow, cupped,* *double (35 petals),* *4" wide, in large clusters,* *recurrent*	**Buds:** *globular* **Flowers:** *orange-pink,* *double (33 petals),* *3.5–4" wide,* *1–5 in a cluster, recurrent*
Fragrance: *very strong Damask*	**Fragrance:** *very strong*	**Fragrance:** *strong*
Foliage: *light green;* *new growth green tinged red* **Height:** *4' with similar spread*	**Foliage:** *light green, semiglossy;* *new growth light green* *tinged red* **Height:** *4–7' upright,* *bushy growth*	**Foliage:** *dark green, glossy;* *new growth medium green* *tinged red* **Height:** *3–4' spreading,* *bushy growth*
Disease resistance: *good*	**Disease resistance:** *good*	**Disease resistance:** *good*

'MARY ROSE'
—*Shrub (seedling× 'The Friar')*
1983

'SIR WALTER RALEIGH'
—*Shrub ('Lilian Austin'×*
'Chaucer') 1985

'MME ISAAC PEREIRE'
(selection of R. borboniana*)*
1881

Hybridizer: *David Austin,*
Austin Roses, Albrighton,
England

Hybridizer: *David Austin,*
Austin Roses, Albrighton,
England

Selected by *M. Garçon, Rouen,*
Seine-Inférieure, France

Buds: *globular*
Flowers: *medium pink,*
double (40+ petals),
3.5–4" wide, cupped,
recurrent

Buds: *pointed*
Flowers: *creamy pink,*
double (40+ petals),
recurrent

Buds: *short, pointed*
Flowers: *deep rose-pink,*
shaded purple, very double,
quartered, somewhat recurrent

Fragrance: *strong Damask*

Fragrance: *strong*

Fragrance: *very strong*

Foliage: *medium green;*
new growth medium red,
semiglossy
Height: *4–5' upright,*
bushy growth

Foliage: *large, medium green;*
new growth light green,
glossy; prickles deep red
Height: *4' upright,*
bushy growth

Foliage: *dark green, semiglossy*
Height: *5–6'*
bushy, spreading growth

Disease resistance: *good*

Disease resistance: *good*

Disease resistance: *good*

BOURBON

'ZÉPHIRINE DROUHIN'
(parentage unknown) 1868

Selected by *Bizot, France*

Buds: *long, pointed*
Flowers: *rose with a white base, semidouble (12+ petals), 3.5–4" wide, cupped, recurrent*

Fragrance: *very strong*

Foliage: *light green, soft, canes have few or no prickles*
Height: *8–12', can be used as climber*

Disease resistance: *good*

CENTIFOLIA

'FANTIN LATOUR'
(parentage and date unknown; named after French painter Henri Fantin-Latour)

Buds: *ovoid*
Flowers: *silvery pink, very double (200 petals), 3–3.5" wide, button-centered, nonrecurrent*

Fragrance: *very strong*

Foliage: *dark green, smooth, semiglossy*
Height: *5–6' upright, vigorous growth*

Disease resistance: *good*

DAMASK

R. × DAMASCENA TRIGINTIPETALA
(Rose of Kazanlik)
(date unknown)

Buds: *ovoid*
Flowers: *clear pink, double (30 petals), 3–4" wide, recurrent*

Fragrance: *very strong—the essence attar of roses is extracted from the flowers*

Foliage: *medium to dark green*
Height: *6–7' bushy, vigorous growth*

Disease resistance: *good*

GALLICA	GALLICA	GALLICA

'CAMAIEUX' *(parentage unknown) 1830*	**'CHARLES DE MILLS'** *(parentage and date unknown)*	**'COMPLICATA'** *(parentage and date unknown; possibly a hybrid of R. × macrantha)*
Buds: *ovoid* **Flowers:** *pink with stripes that are red, purple, or rose fading to white with purple stripes, double (50 petals), 3–3.5" wide, cupped, camellia-like, nonrecurrent*	**Buds:** *short, stocky* **Flowers:** *dark crimson and purple, very double (150+ petals), 3.5–4.5" wide, quartered, nonrecurrent*	**Buds:** *large, pointed* **Flowers:** *deep pink with a white eye, single (5 petals), 4.5" wide, nonrecurrent*
Fragrance: *very strong*	**Fragrance:** *strong*	**Fragrance:** *strong*
Foliage: *medium green* **Height:** *3–4' upright, rounded habit*	**Foliage:** *medium green, rough* **Height:** *to 5' upright, vigorous growth*	**Foliage:** *large, soft, medium green; few thorns; attractive large red hips* **Height:** *5–7' arching canes, vigorous*
Disease resistance: *good*	**Disease resistance:** *good*	**Disease resistance:** *good*

GALLICA	HYBRID MACRANTHA	HYBRID MUSK
R. GALLICA *'VERSICOLOR'* *("Rosa Mundi") (before 1581)*	**'RAUBRITTER'** *('Daisy Hill' × 'Solarium') 1936*	**'BALLERINA'** *(seedling) 1937*
	Hybridizer: *Kordes, Germany*	**Selected by** *Ann J. Bentall, Havering Romford, Essex, England*
Buds: *ovoid* **Flowers:** *medium to deep pink with white striping, semidouble (18–24 petals), 3–3.5" wide, cupped, nonrecurrent*	**Buds:** *short, pointed* **Flowers:** *light pink, semidouble (12–15 petals), 2–3" wide, globular in clusters, nonrecurrent*	**Buds:** *small, pointed* **Flowers:** *soft pink with white eye, bright, single (5 petals), 2" wide, very large clusters, recurrent*
Fragrance: *strong*	**Fragrance:** *mild*	**Fragrance:** *slight musk*
Foliage: *medium green; bloodred hips* **Height:** *3–3.5' upright, bush*	**Foliage:** *grayish to medium green, leathery, wrinkled* **Height:** *3–6' trailing, bushy growth*	**Foliage:** *light green, glossy* **Height:** *3–5' dense, spreading growth*
Disease resistance: *good*	**Disease resistance:** *good*	**Disease resistance:** *good*

HYBRID MUSK	**HYBRID MUSK**	**HYBRID MUSK**

'BELINDA' *(parentage unknown) 1936*	**'BUFF BEAUTY'** *('William Allen Richardson' ×* *seedling) 1939*	**'LAVENDER LASSIE'** *(parentage unknown;* *possibly a hybrid of* R. moschata*) 1960*
Hybridizer: *Ann J. Bentall,* *Havering Romford, Essex,* *England*	**Hybridizer:** *Ann J. Bentall,* *Havering Romford, Essex,* *England*	**Hybridizer:** *Kordes,* *Germany*
Buds: *ovoid* **Flowers:** *medium pink,* *semidouble (12–15 petals),* *1–2" wide, very large* *erect trusses, recurrent*	**Buds:** *ovoid* **Flowers:** *apricot-yellow,* *double (50 petals), 4" wide,* *in clusters up to 12, recurrent*	**Buds:** *ovoid* **Flowers:** *lilac-pink, double* *(20+ petals), 3" wide,* *large clusters, recurrent*
Fragrance: *light*	**Fragrance:** *strong*	**Fragrance:** *strong*
Foliage: *light green,* *semiglossy* **Height:** *4–6' bushy,* *spreading, vigorous habit*	**Foliage:** *large, medium green,* *semiglossy;* *new growth bronze-tinted* **Height:** *to 6' bushy,* *spreading habit*	**Foliage:** *dark green;* *new growth bronze-tinted* **Height:** *5' upright,* *vigorous growth*
Disease resistance: *good*	**Disease resistance:** *good*	**Disease resistance:** *good*

HYBRID RUGOSA	HYBRID RUGOSA	HYBRID RUGOSA
'FRAU DAGMAR HARTOPP' ('Frau Dagmar Hastrup') (R. rugosa *seedling*) 1914	**'ROSERAIE DE L'HAY'** (*possible sport of* R. rugosa 'Rubra') 1900	**'SARAH VAN FLEET'** (*reportedly* R. rugosa × 'My Maryland') 1926
	Introduced by *Cochet-Cochet, Coubert, Seine-et-Marne, France*	**Hybridizer:** *Dr. Walter Van Fleet, Glen Dale, Md.*
Buds: *pointed* **Flowers:** *silvery pink, single (5 petals), recurrent*	**Buds:** *long, pointed* **Flowers:** *crimson red opening to rosy magenta, double (20+ petals), 4–5" wide, recurrent*	**Buds:** *short, pointed* **Flowers:** *rose-pink, semidouble (18–24 petals), 3–3.5" wide, cupped, recurrent*
Fragrance: *light*	**Fragrance:** *very strong*	**Fragrance:** *strong*
Foliage: *deep green, crinkled, rugose; large red hips in fall* **Height:** *1–4', growing wider than tall*	**Foliage:** *dark green, rugose* **Height:** *4–6' upright, vigorous growth*	**Foliage:** *olive green, leathery, rugose* **Height:** *6–8' upright, vigorous growth*
Disease resistance: *good*	**Disease resistance:** *good*	**Disease resistance:** *good*

HYBRID RUGOSA	**HYBRID RUGOSA**	**HYBRID SPINOSISSIMA**

'SIR THOMAS LIPTON' (R. rugosa 'Alba' × 'Clotilde Soupert') 1900	**'THÉRÈSE BUGNET'** ([R. acicularis × R. rugosa 'Kamtchatica'] × [R. amblyotis × R. rugosa 'Plena'] × 'Betty Bland') 1950	**'STANWELL PERPETUAL'** (thought to be a repeat-blooming Damask × R. spinosissima hybrid) 1838
Hybridizer: Dr. William Van Fleet, Glen Dale, Md.	**Hybridizer:** George Bugnet, Canada	**Introduced by** Lee, Hammersmith, England
Buds: long, pointed **Flowers:** white, double (20–25 petals), 2.5–3″ wide, cupped, recurrent	**Buds:** conical, sharp-tipped **Flowers:** red aging to pale pink, double (35 petals), 4″ wide, recurrent	**Buds:** short, pointed **Flowers:** blush pink, double (20–30 petals), 1.5–2″ wide, recurrent
Fragrance: strong	**Fragrance:** strong	**Fragrance:** mild
Foliage: dark green, leathery **Height:** 4–8′ upright growth; tolerant of poor soil	**Foliage:** dark green coloring to red in fall; colorful red canes in winter **Height:** 6′ upright, vase-shaped	**Foliage:** medium gray-green, very small **Height:** 5′ spreading growth, suckering with many small prickles
Disease resistance: good	**Disease resistance:** good	**Disease resistance:** good

MOSS	MOSS	PORTLAND
'CRESTED MOSS' (*'Chapeau de Napoléon'*) (*found on wall of convent near Fribourg, Switzerland*) 1827	**'HENRI MARTIN'** (*'Red Moss'*) (*parentage unknown*) 1863	**'JACQUES CARTIER'** (*'Marchesa Boccella'*) (*parentage unknown; probably a Portland× Damask hybrid*) 1868
	Hybridizer: *M. Laffay, Bellevue, France*	***Introduced by*** *Robert Moreau*
Buds: *triangular with moss confined to edges of sepals* ***Flowers:*** *pink, very double (200 petals), 3–3.5" wide, nonrecurrent*	***Buds:*** *sparsely mossed* ***Flowers:*** *dark crimson, double (65–75 petals), round, 2.5" wide in clusters of 3–8, nonrecurrent*	***Buds:*** *ovoid* ***Flowers:*** *clear rose with darker center, very double (50+ petals), 4–4.5" wide, quartered, recurrent*
Fragrance: *very strong*	***Fragrance:*** *strong*	***Fragrance:*** *very strong*
Foliage: *dull, medium green, rough* ***Height:*** *5–7' upright, arching, open habit*	***Foliage:*** *medium to dark green* ***Height:*** *5' upright, bushy growth*	***Foliage:*** *dark green* ***Height:*** *3' compact, bushy growth*
Disease resistance: *good*	***Disease resistance:*** *good*	***Disease resistance:*** *good*

SPECIES

SPECIES

R. GLAUCA
(R. rubrifolia) *pre-1830*

R. MOYESII
Introduced in 1903 by E.H. Wilson from western China; named for missonary J. Moyes

Buds: *short, pointed* **Flowers:** *light to medium pink, single (5 petals), 1.5" wide, singly or in 3–5's, nonrecurrent*	**Buds:** *short, pointed* **Flowers:** *deep bloodred through deep rose to light pink, single (5 petals), 1.75–2.5" wide, singly or in 2's, hips oblong-ovoid, deep orange-red, appearing in summer; nonrecurrent*
Fragrance: *little to none*	**Fragrance:** *little to none*
Foliage: *gray-green to red-purple; purple fall color; canes red; hips red, subglobose* **Height:** *to 6' upright, sparsely caned growth*	**Foliage:** *deep green, delicate, compound (up to 13 leaflets)* **Height:** *10–13'*
Disease resistance: *good*	**Disease resistance:** *good*

Rosa Indica   *Grande Indienne.*

APPENDIX:
THE BEST AND
THE WORST

lthough the expertise of NYBG is invaluable, there is no substitute for local experience in matters pertaining to roses. What follows are the results of an informal survey of 27 public rose gardens across the United States about the roses that performed best in those gardens, together with a summary of the most troublesome pests and diseases.

Often the most interesting information to emerge from each rose garden's report is not the exact varieties that perform best there but the classes that supply these stars. Gardeners in, for example, Montana may not find the orange-flowered Miniature rose 'Pucker Up' to their taste, but when they find that five out of the ten most reliable roses in the local garden are Miniatures, they would be wise to consider this class when shopping for their own landscape.

Accordingly, the name of each rose variety in the following lists is preceded by an abbreviation of the class to which that rose belongs. The key to these abbreviations appears on page 184.

ABBREVIATIONS

Cl Pol	Climbing Polyantha
D	Damask
E	Eglanteria
F	Floribunda
Gr	Grandiflora
HMsk	Hybrid Musk
HP	Hybrid Perpetual
HRg	Hybrid Rugosa
HT	Hybrid Tea
K	Kordesii
LCl	Large-flowered Climbing
Min	Miniature
Pol	Polyantha
S	Shrub
Sp	Species

CALIFORNIA

PAGEANT OF ROSES GARDEN
3900 South Workman Mill Rd.
Whittier, CA
310-692-1212
6,000 plants, 600 varieties

1. HT 'Brigadoon'
2. HT 'Double Delight'
3. HT 'First Prize'
4. HT 'Miss All-American Beauty'
5. HT 'Mr. Lincoln'
6. HT 'Olympiad'
7. HT 'Paloma'
8. HT 'Princesse de Monaco'
9. Gr 'Arizona'
10. Gr 'Tournament of Roses'
11. F 'Showbiz'
12. F 'Sunsprite'

Problems: Rust, powdery mildew, aphids, thrips, spider mites

COLORADO

LONGMONT MEMORIAL ROSE GARDEN Roosevelt
Park , 700 Longs Peak
Longmont, CO 80501
303-651-8446
1,300 plants, 100 varieties

1. HT 'Double Delight'
2. HT 'Midas Touch'
3. HT 'Milestone'
4. HT 'Olympiad'
5. HT 'Secret'
6. HT 'Touch of Class'
7. HT 'Yankee Doodle'
8. Gr 'Caribbean'
9. Gr 'Tournament of Roses'
10. F 'Iceberg'

Problems: Powdery mildew, blackspot

IDAHO

JULIA DAVIS ROSE GARDEN
Julia Davis Dr.
Boise, ID 83706
208-384-4327
2,000 plants, 200 varieties

1. HT 'Chicago Peace'
2. HT 'Electron'
3. HT 'Mr. Lincoln'
4. HT 'Peace'
5. HT 'Promise'
6. HT 'Touch of Class'
7. HT 'Tropicana'
8. Gr 'Gold Medal'
9. Gr 'Love'
10. F 'Cherish'

Problems: Spider mites, blackspot, powdery mildew

ILLINOIS

GEORGE L. LUTHY MEMORIAL ROSE GARDEN
2218 North Prospect Rd.
Peoria, IL 61603
309-686-3362
800 plants, 107 varieties

1. HT 'Double Delight'
2. HT 'Mr. Lincoln'
3. HT 'Oregold'
4. HT 'Olympiad'
5. HT 'Peace'
6. HT 'Tropicana'
7. F 'Angel Face'
8. S 'Carefree Delight'
9. S 'Carefree Wonder'
10. Sp R. rugosa 'Rubra'

Problems: Deer, blackspot, Japanese beetles

CONNECTICUT	FLORIDA	GEORGIA

**ELIZABETH PARK
ROSE GARDEN**
150 Walbridge Rd.
West Hartford, CT 06119
203-722-6543
15,000 plants, 800 varieties

1. HT 'Cary Grant'
2. HT 'Earth Song'
3. HT 'Garden Party'
4. HT 'Jardins de Bagatelle'
5. HT 'Perfume Delight'
6. Gr 'Love'
7. F 'Old Master'
8. Min 'Antique Rose'
9. S 'Carefree Beauty'
10. S 'Carefree Wonder'
11. S 'Scarlet Meilland'
12. HP 'General Washington'

Problems: Blackspot, spider mites, thrips, Japanese beetles

**STURGEON MEMORIAL
ROSE GARDEN**
13401 Indian River Rocks Rd.
Largo, FL 34644
813-595-2914
850 plants, 125 varieties

1. HT 'Double Delight'
2. HT 'Oklahoma'
3. LCl 'Don Juan'
4. HT 'American Pride'
5. HT 'Kentucky Derby'
6. HT 'John F. Kennedy'
7. F 'Angel Face'
8. F 'French Lace'
9. F 'Ivory Fashion'
10. HT 'Peace'

Problems: Aphids, blackspot, nematodes

**ATLANTA BOTANICAL
GARDEN**
Piedmont Park at the Prado
Atlanta, GA 30309
404-876-5859
730 plants, 47 varieties

1. HT 'Double Delight'
2. HT 'First Prize'
3. HT 'Olympiad'
4. HT 'Peace'
5. HT 'Touch of Class'
6. Gr 'Queen Elizabeth'
7. F 'Angel Face'
8. F 'Betty Prior'
9. F 'Europeana'
10. F 'Sunsprite'
11. S 'Mary Rose'

Problems: Blackspot, powdery mildew, aphids, spider mites

INDIANA	IOWA	KANSAS

RICHMOND ROSE GARDEN
Glen Miller Park
2500 National Rd. East
Richmond, IN 47374
317-966-3425
2,000 plants, 100 varieties

1. HT 'Mr. Lincoln'
2. HT 'Olympiad'
3. HT 'Peace'
4. Gr 'Queen Elizabeth'
5. F 'Angel Face'
6. F 'Betty Prior'
7. F 'Europeana'
8. S 'Bonica'

Problems: Japanese beetles, blackspot

**VANDER VEER PARK
MUNICIPAL ROSE GARDEN**
215 West Central Park Ave.
Davenport, IA 52803
319-326-7818
2,000 plants, 170 varieties

1. HT 'Chicago Peace'
2. HT 'Double Delight'
3. HT 'Midas Touch'
4. HT 'Miss All-American Beauty'
5. HT 'Rio Samba'
6. HT 'White Delight'
7. F 'Showbiz'
8. S 'All That Jazz'
9. S 'Graham Thomas'
10. S 'Heritage'

Problems: Blackspot, spider mites, winter cold

**E.F.A. REINISCH
ROSE GARDEN** Gage Park,
4320 West Tenth St.
Topeka, KS 66604
913-272-6150
6,500 plants, 400 varieties

1. HT 'Brigadoon'
2. HT 'Dainty Bess'
3. HT 'Olympiad'
4. HT 'Princesse de Monaco'
5. HT 'Rio Samba'
6. HT 'Touch of Class'
7. Gr 'Queen Elizabeth'
8. Gr 'Shining Hour'
9. F 'Sweet Vivian'
10. LCl 'America'
11. LCl 'Red Fountain'

Problems: Spider mites, blackspot, powdery mildew

KENTUCKY

KENTUCKY PUBLIC ROSE GARDEN
Kentucky Fair & Exposition Ctr.
Louisville, KY 40232
502-267-6308
1,500 plants, 98 varieties

1. S 'Carefree Delight'
2. F 'Showbiz'
3. HT 'Double Delight'
4. Gr 'Queen Elizabeth'
5. Min 'New Beginning'
6. Min 'Pride 'n' Joy'
7. HT 'Brigadoon'
8. F 'Betty Prior'

Problems: *Japanese beetles, blackspot, powdery mildew*

MAINE

CITY OF PORTLAND ROSE CIRCLE
Deering Oaks Park, High St. Ext.
Portland, ME 04101
207-874-8461
550 plants, 38 varieties

1. HT 'Peace'
2. HT 'Chicago Peace'
3. S 'Carefree Wonder'
4. HT 'Double Delight'
5. Gr 'Love'
6. HT 'Mikado'
7. Gr 'Queen Elizabeth'
8. HT 'Paradise'
9. HT 'Pristine'
10. F 'Showbiz'

MASSACHUSETTS

JAMES P. KELLEHER ROSE GARDEN
Park Dr.
Boston, MA 04101
617-635-7381
550 plants, 38 varieties

1. HT 'John F. Kennedy'
2. HT 'South Seas'
3. HT 'Royal Highness'
4. HT 'White Knight'
5. HT 'American Heritage'
6. HT 'Lady X'
7. HT 'Miss All-American Beauty'
8. HT 'Granada'
9. HT 'Fragrant Cloud'
10. HT 'Chicago Peace'

MONTANA

MISSOULA MEMORIAL ROSE GARDEN
Blaine & Brooks Sts.
Missoula, MT 59833
406-273-0061
950 plants, 75 varieties

1. S 'Lavender Dream'
2. HT 'Pascali'
3. Min 'Elaina'
4. S 'Golden Wings'
5. HT 'Chrysler Imperial'
6. Min 'Minnie Pearl'
7. HT 'Lady X'
8. Min 'Pucker Up'
9. Min 'New Beginning'
10. Min 'Popcorn'

Problems: *Blackspot, powdery mildew, aphids, spider mites*

NEBRASKA

BOYS TOWN AARS CONSTITUTION ROSE GARDEN
Father Flanagan's Boys Home
Boys Town, NE 68010
402-498-1104
1,500+ plants, 30+ varieties

1. HT 'American Pride'
2. HT 'Cayenne'
3. HT 'Chrysler Imperial'
4. HT 'Dolly Parton'
5. HT 'Double Delight'
6. HT 'Dynasty'
7. HT 'Friendship'
8. HT 'Las Vegas'
9. HT 'Love'
10. HT 'Rio Samba'
11. F 'Interama'

Problems: *Powdery mildew, blackspot*

NEVADA

RENO MUNICIPAL ROSE GARDEN
2055 Idlewild Dr.
Reno, NV 89509
702-334-2270
2,400 plants, 560 varieties

1. HT 'Candy Stripe'
2. HT 'Chicago Peace'
3. HT 'Olympiad'
4. HT 'Oregold'
5. HT 'Tropicana'
6. F 'Betty Prior'
7. F 'Europeana'
8. F 'Iceberg'
9. F 'Pleasure'
10. LCl 'Don Juan'

Problems: *Powdery mildew, canker, fire blight, aphids*

MINNESOTA

LYNDALE PARK MUNICIPAL ROSE GARDEN
4125 East Lake Harriet Parkway
Minneapolis, MN 55409
612-348-4448
3,000 plants, 450 varieties

1. F 'Nearly Wild'
2. S 'Adelaide Hoodless'
3. S 'Carefree Wonder'
4. S 'Morden Blush'
5. S 'Morden Centennial'
6. K 'Henry Kelsey'
7. K 'William Baffin'
8. HRg 'David Thompson'
9. HRg 'Thérèse Bugnet'

Problems: Powdery mildew, blackspot, spider mites

MISSISSIPPI

THE JIM BUCK ROSS ROSE GARDEN
1150 Lakeland Dr.
Jackson, MS 39216
601-354-6113
1,100 plants, 180 varieties

1. HT 'Tiffany'
2. HT 'Mr. Lincoln'
3. HT 'Peace'
4. HT 'Double Delight'
5. HT 'Pristine'
6. Gr 'Queen Elizabeth'
7. F 'Iceberg'
8. Pol 'The Fairy'
9. Cl Pol 'Cécile Brünner'
10. LCl 'Altissimo'

Problems: Spider mites, blackspot, powdery mildew, thrips

MISSOURI

GLADWAY & LEHMANN ROSE GARDEN
4344 Shaw Blvd.
St. Louis, MO 63110
314-577-5190
4,000 plants, 250 varieties

1. HT 'Brides Dream'
2. Gr 'Camelot'
3. F 'Iceberg'
4. F 'Sweet Vivian'
5. Min 'Pride 'n' Joy'
6. S 'Bonica'
7. S 'Constance Spry'
8. S 'Country Dancer'
9. S 'Nearly Wild'
10. S 'William Baffin'
11. HMsk 'Ballerina'
12. E 'Magnifica'

Problems: Powdery mildew, aphids, blackspot

NEW HAMPSHIRE

FULLER GARDENS ROSE GARDEN
10 Willow Ave.
North Hampton, NH 03862
603-964-5414
1,700 plants, 150 varieties

1. HT 'Legend'
2. HT 'Garden Party'
3. HT 'Touch of Class'
4. HT 'Paradise'
5. Gr 'Queen Elizabeth'
6. Gr 'Carousel'
7. Gr 'Love'
8. F 'Lilli Marleen'
9. F 'Sexy Rexy'
10. F 'Iceberg'
11. Min 'Gourmet Popcorn'

Problems: Rose midge, mildew, leaf hoppers, spider mites, rust

NORTH CAROLINA

THE BILTMORE ESTATE
1 Biltmore Plaza
Asheville, NC 28803
704-274-6246
1,992 plants, 175 varieties

1. HT 'Mr. Lincoln'
2. HT 'Rio Samba'
3. HT 'Secret'
4. HT 'Sweet Surrender'
5. Gr 'Queen Elizabeth'
6. Cl Pol 'Climbing Cécile Brünner'
7. S 'Bonica'
8. S 'Sea Foam'
9. Pol 'Cécile Brünner'

Problems: Powdery mildew, spider mites, blackspot

OHIO

COLUMBUS PARK OF ROSES
3923 North High St.
Columbus, OH 43214
614-645-6648
10,952 plants, 372 varieties

1. HT 'Fascination'
2. HT 'Love'
3. Gr 'Camelot'
4. Gr 'Lagerfeld'
5. F 'Evening Star'
6. F 'Impatient'
7. F 'Lilli Marleen'
8. F 'Marina'
9. F 'Sunsprite'
10. F 'Viva'

Problems: Blackspot, powdery mildew, Japanese beetle

OKLAHOMA

**TULSA MUNICIPAL
ROSE GARDEN**
*Woodward Park, 21st & Peoria
Tulsa, OK 74114
918-746-5155
9,000 plants, 256 varieties*

1. HT 'Mon Cheri'
2. HT 'Olympiad'
3. HT 'Mr. Lincoln'
4. HT 'Perfume Delight'
5. S 'Carefree Wonder'
6. S 'Bonica'
7. Gr 'Shining Hour'
8. Min 'Pride 'n' Joy'
9. F 'Betty Prior'
10. F 'Angel Face'

PENNSYLVANIA

HERSHEY GARDENS
*P.O. Box 416, Hotel Rd.
Hershey, PA 17033
717-534-3493
8,000 plants, 275 varieties*

1. HT 'Chrysler Imperial'
2. HT 'Garden Party'
3. HT 'Gold Medal'
4. HT 'Mr. Lincoln'
5. HT 'Olympiad'
6. HT 'Secret'
7. HT 'Sheer Bliss'
8. Gr 'Queen Elizabeth'
9. LCl 'New Dawn'
10. HP 'American Beauty'

Problems: *Blackspot, aphids,
spider mites*

VIRGINIA

**NORFOLK BOTANICAL
GARDEN**
*Bicentennial Rose Garden
Norfolk, VA 23518
804-441-5830
3,000 plants, 280 varieties*

1. HT 'Color Magic'
2. HT 'Double Delight'
3. HT 'Dolly Parton'
4. HT 'Electron'
5. HT 'First Prize'
6. HT 'Headliner'
7. HT 'Love'
8. HT 'Peace'
9. HT 'Pristine'
10. HT 'Olympiad'
11. HT 'Secret'
12. HT 'Tiffany'

Problems: *Powdery mildew,
aphids, spider mites*

WASHINGTON

MANITO PARK–ROSE HILL
*4 West 21st Ave.
Spokane, WA 99203
509-625-6622
1,500+ plants, 141 varieties*

1. HT 'Dainty Bess'
2. HT 'Electron'
3. HT 'Kentucky Derby'
4. HT 'Pascali'
5. HT 'Peter Frankenfeld'
6. HT 'Summer Sunshine'
7. Gr 'Camelot'
8. Gr 'Scarlet Knight'
9. F 'All Gold'
10. F 'Arthur Bell'
11. F 'Europeana'

WEST VIRGINIA

THE PALACE ROSE GARDEN
*RD 1, Box 319
Moundsville, WV 26041
304-845-4175
2,000 plants, 100 varieties*

1. HT 'Chrysler Imperial'
2. HT 'Garden Party'
3. HT 'Mr. Lincoln'
4. F 'Europeana'
5. F 'Regenberg'
6. LCl 'Coral Dawn'
7. LCl 'Galway Bay'
8. Min 'Little Red Devil'
9. Min 'Magic Carrousel'
10. Min 'Pink Bounty'

Problems: *Spider mites,
midges, blackspot*